Dr. Janko Prunk

A BRIEF HISTORY OF SLOVENIA

HISTORICAL BACKGROUND OF
THE REPUBLIC OF SLOVENIA

ZALOŽBA GRAD

LJUBLJANA

CIP - Kataložni zapis o publikaciji
Narodna in univerzitetna knjižnica, Ljubljana

94(497.4)

PRUNK, Janko
    A Brief History of Slovenia: historical background of the
Republic of Slovenia / Janko Prunk; (translated by Wayne
Tuttle, Majda Klander ; foreword by Borut Šuklje). - Ljubljana
: Založba Grad, 1996

ISBN 961-90119-2-9

59839488

FOREWORD

On the political map of Europe and the world, Slovenia may be a new and unfamiliar concept for many since after winning its political independence in 1991 it has been only slowly making its way toward wider recognition by Europe and the world through numerous and increasingly extensive economic, scientific, cultural, athletic, tourist, and, of course, political contacts and links.

The formation of Slovene nationhood and the Slovene state, fostered by aspirations of social and economic democratization, has been a long and uneven process hindered by numerous divisions and appropriations of Slovene territory and the subjugation of its population by more powerful neighbours and European superpowers since feudal times when the centers of political, economic, and ideological power have always been outside Slovene territory. As a result, the Slovenes could only assert themselves ethnically, initially as a cultural entity and only much later as a political and state-forming community, even though they already had entirely recognizable and historically proven origins toward the end of the first millennium.

By persistently resisting absolutist and hegemonic pressure from outside. the Slovenes gradually widened their sphere of freedom, and it is possible to follow the conscious stream of this continuous process from the Reformation and Counter-Reformation all the way to the worst unconcealed genocidal experiences of World War II. After several centuries of Hapsburg domination, from which the Slovenes wrested themselves only after World War I, and after seventy years of uncomfortable and in many ways subservient and repressed coexistence in the former Yugoslav states, the awareness ripened among the Slovenes of the need for complete and absolute independence in order to manage their internal social, economic, and political life according to democratic European standards and to be fully entitled to involve themselves in present and future streams of European development.

In this book, history as an interwoven sequence of individual events, developmental stages, accidental and deliberate circumstances, and particular facts is not intended to serve any violent reconstruction of a glorious and mighty past that would substantiate the current historical legitimacy of the Slovene state or to assert some sort of teleological determination of the present situation. This historical survey of events only wishes to call attention to the fact that the territory inhabited by the Slovenes today cannot in the European space and consciousness be viewed as marginal and that it is by no means a "white spot" or a "blank sheet of paper" as some particular aspects taken out of the wider context might suggest.

This insight into the Slovene past can in many ways throw light on the goals and aspirations of today's citizens of Slovenia and of their state and their society. Slovenia's geographical, political, and strategic position dictates that they carefully follow events in the international arena and become involved through their best achievements in all spheres of economic, social, political, scientific, and cultural life with openness to ideas and suggestions coming from elsewhere and with the assertion of their own ideas and suggestions outward. This orientation was established by the plebiscite preceding independence five years ago and has been confirmed in the form of a dynamic democratic transformation of the social and economic system accompanied by special concern for the political and social rights of the individual and for the optimal development of its intellectual, cultural, and creative potential. In view of the considerable economic success and demonstrable breakthroughs in numerous other fields, the rapid transformation that has occurred in the last five years is confirmation that this orientation is correct and guarantees that the world can find in Slovenia an attractive, reliable, and cooperative partner for the numerous joint ventures that will mark our common future.

A Brief History of Slovenia is intended for foreigners visiting the Republic of Slovenia and for all those who have some small contact with it as tourists, economists, politicians, scholars, or artists. It offers a basic survey of the historical development of Slovenia and tries to fill the acute gap due to the lack of suitable literature in foreign languages. We are certain and we hope that this book will be followed by many others.

Borut Šuklje
Government Information Office

INTRODUCTION

The Republic of Slovenia is an independent state on territory settled by the Slovene nation that came into existence after the dissolution of the Federative Republic of Yugoslavia in 1991. The Slovene nation is a special ethnic entity within the Slav language group.

The Slav ethnos prevailed in the region of present-day Slovenia and in some bordering countries until the end of the 6th century. Through the centuries, from the period of the Reformation to the beginning of the 19th century, the Slovene nation was formed from this Slav ethnos.

Slovenia encompasses 20,256 km^2 and has a population just over two million. Over 90% of its inhabitants are Slovenes, the old Italian and Hungarian minorities living in areas bordering on Italy and Hungary make up 1%, and the remainder are members of other Yugoslav nations who settled in Slovenia in the last decades when Slovenia was still a member of the Yugoslav state. A part of the Slovene nation is autochthonous in areas of Austria, Italy, and Hungary bordering on Slovenia.

The territory of present-day Slovenia lies in the south of Central Europe between the southeastern margin of the Alps and the Northern Adriatic. In the west it borders on the northern Italian flatlands, in the east it opens toward the Pannonian Plain, and in the southeast toward the Balkan Dinaric Alps. Throughout history this territory has had a distinctly crossroads character, linking Central Europe with the Mediterranean and the Balkan

Peninsula and Italy with the Pannonian Plain. More than half of the territory is mountainous and partly of karstic character. There is little rich fertile land suitable for successful cultivation, and from the beginnings of civilization (from the Late Iron Age represented by the Celtic state of Noricum in the last centuries B.C.) the population of this territory has consequently been forced to a large extent to be engaged in nonagricultural production. The specific location of this territory has also been reflected in its geopolitical fate.

Independent political units centered in this area have only rarely succeeded in developing and surviving, and other stronger national political formations in the region have always tried to appropriate this strategically important region to reinforce their geostrategic position. This territory has therefore always been included in the hegemonic force of European civilizations of particular times which then spread their civilizations over this territory in their direct form only a little later. Thus, after the fall at the end of the 2nd century B.C. of the Celtic state of Noricum that had its center in this area, this territory fell under Roman influence, where it remained until the fall of the Roman Empire in the time of the great migration of nations.

In this period at the end of the 6th century, the Slav ethnos prevailed in the territory of present-day Slovenia and considerably farther north in the present-day Austrian provinces of Carinthia, East Tyrol, and Styria, as well as on the eastern margin of the Italian state, in Istria, and in western Hungary. At the beginning of the 7th century, the Slav ethnos formed the tribal state of Karantanija in the territory of present-day Austrian Carinthia and probably also the tribal principality of Carniola south of the Karavanke Mountains in the Sava River watershed. At the end of the 8th century, after they had existed as independent states for a century and a half, these two Slav state formations were incorporated in the Frankish state and later in its successor the Holy Roman Empire. From the 14th century until 1918, the territory of Slovenia had the status of hereditary province under the Hapsburgs, who had the center of their empire again outside Slovenia – in Vienna. Only in the first half of the 15th century was a sort of independent state established in the center of Slovene territory: the Celje Principality that was a direct member of the Holy Roman Empire and led a boldly conceived independent foreign policy of wider Central European and Balkan connections. When the Celje dynasty died out, their legacy fell again to the Hapsburgs. From the early Middle Ages until the beginning of the 20th century, under foreign rulers and foreign centers of government in political states where they were among the smallest groups, the Slovenes lost to a great extent the original ethnic territory they had occupied at the beginning of the Middle Ages when Karantanija existed. They suffered the greatest losses in the north to the German ethnos, while the ethnic border with the Romanic peoples that formed along the Lombard limes remained almost unchanged until the 20th century.

During the period of the Reformation in the 16th century, the Slovene ethnos began to form itself culturally into a nation, and by the period of the Enlightenment, the Slovene national awakening could be based on social, economic, legal, and political bases of enlightened civilized action.

A modern national consciousness developed among the Slovenes until the middle of the 19th century at which time the nation established its own national political program to unite all the provinces occupied by Slovenes into a single unit that would enjoy national and political autonomy within the Hapsburg Monarchy. At the end of the 19th century, the majority of Slovene nation, by this time a completely developed national entity, was aroused by this program.

Because Slovene nation had failed to realize national-political autonomy within the Hapsburg Monarchy and believing that prospects for its national development would be more easily secured, it decided to leave the Austrian Empire at the end of World War I and establish the Yugoslav state together with the Serbs and Croats. In its three quarters of a century within this state, the Slovene nation developed its existence considerably, as well as its political awareness of the necessity of having its own national state.

In the new civilizational paradigm of the last decade of the 20th century, the Slovene nation decided to leave Yugoslavia, which had become an obstacle to its further civilizational development. It proclaimed the independent Republic of Slovenia and sought its place in the European Union.

I. THE ANCESTORS OF THE PRESENT-DAY SLOVENES

1. The Territory of Present-day Slovenia in Pre-Roman and Roman Times

We have very few traces of human habitation in this area from the Paleolithic period, but there are numerous archeological finds witnessing the life of man in the Neolithic period in the area between the karst and the Pannonian Plain. A feature of this period were the numerous human crannog dwellings in the Ljubljana Barje (the Ljubljana Moor) area which was then a lake.

The Early Iron Age or Hallstatt period that lasted from the 8th to the 4th century B.C. witnessed a great rise in settlement and in the quality of life on Slovene territory. According to archeological finds, this period ranks at the very peak of Hallstatt culture in Central Europe (e.g., the *Vače situla*). During this period agriculture and the casting of iron flourished. In a decided way the tribal society was already disintegrating, and from it rose a higher social class, the military aristocracy led by princes. Human habitations acquired new locations and new forms, primarily on hills that were fortified for defence. Hallstatt settlements stretched from the Soča region (Most na Soči) across the central part of Slovenia (Vače) as far as eastern Slovene areas around Rifnik, Stična, and Novo mesto. The bearers of this culture have not been precisely identified except in the eastern areas where Illyrian tribes are believed to have settled.

The Late Iron Age La Tene culture was brought to Slovene territory in the 4th century B.C. by a new people from Western Europe, the Celts. This period lasted approximately three centuries, and for Slovene territory it meant the transition from prehistory to civilization. Written records and minted coins have survived from this period. The most important Celtic tribe in this area was the Norics, who formed a sort of protostate, the Kingdom of Noricum, the first such state in the eastern Alpine area, with its center at Magdalensberg above Maria Saal. Another center of the Noric Kingdom was in the area of present-day Celje where Noric silver coins were minted in the 1st century B.C.

The first contacts of the Noric Kingdom with Rome date from the beginning of the 2nd century B.C. At first contacts were only economic as Italy was very interested in Noric iron. Trade flowed especially through Aquileia, which was founded in 181 B.C. From the end of the 2nd century B.C., the Roman state began military campaigns against the Noric tribes, especially those east of Noricum itself, the Pannonians, Dalmatians, and Japods. Between 35 and 33 B.C. these tribes fought resolutely against Rome but ultimately succumbed to Roman military supremacy. In 10 B.C. Noricum was incorporated into the Roman state without a fight.

The inclusion of present-day Slovene territory in the Roman state meant a new stage in its civilizational development. Roman administration was introduced in the region which was divided into provinces: Noricum, which was divided into northern, coastal, and southern (Mediterranean or Interior) regions; Histria (Istria); and Pannonia (which was later legally divided into Upper and Lower Pannonia). In the provinces urban settlements or *civitas* began to spring up, imposing their administration and authority over extensive agrarian surroundings. Over 150 farmsteads or *villae rusticae* have been discovered in the Slovene countryside.

The first Roman town to develop on the territory of present-day Slovenia was Emona (on the site of present-day Ljubljana), settled by colonists from Aquileia as well as by the veterans of the XVth Roman legion that had its legionary stronghold here. Across the territory of present-day Slovenia the Romans also built the famous roads that they used for moving their legions and for trade. The road running from Aquileia through the Hrušica Pass, Emona, Atrans (Trojane), Celeia (Celje), and Poetovio (Ptuj) to Pannonia was called the *Via Gemina*. Many important settlements sprang up along this road, especially the towns of Celeia and Poetovio, the most important Roman town in Slovene territory. From Emona a road also ran eastwards through present-day Dolenjska past the colony of Noviodunum (Drnovo near Krško) to Siscia (Sisak) in Pannonia.

Occasionally important fortified camps for Roman legions were established on Slovene territory to defend the borders of the Empire on the Danube. Besides the camp of the XVth legion in Emona, the camp of the *Legio II Italicae* at Ločica near Šentpeter in the Savinja Valley was very important, as well as the camp of the *XIIIth Gemina* legion at Poetovio. In this camp, Vespasian was proclaimed Emperor in 69 A.D. In the 3rd century when Germanic tribes began to threaten the Roman Empire, a defense system was built across Slovene territory running from Trsat near Rijeka over the karst passes toward the north as far as the Gail Valley in present-day Austria. The system consisted of fortifications, towers, and valley blockades. The official name of this defense system was *Claustra Alpinum Juliarum*. Historians most often call it simply the *Italian limes*.

Roman might spread Roman civilization over this territory completely. To the administration and economy we have mentioned, it is necessary to add as well the inculturational processes which in this region meant the Romanization of the language. In the last centuries of the Roman Empire, Christianity also spread across Slovene territory, and several diocesan centers are known, including Emona, Virunum (Maria Saal), Celeia, and Poetovio.

The great migration of nations was felt on present-day Slovene territory at the end of the 4th century A.D. when the Visigoths plundered Poetovio in 379. All the barbarian peoples moved across this territory along the road from Emona to Aquileia to invade Italy. In 394, there was a famous battle on the Frigidus River (near present-day Ajdovščina) between the Christian Roman Emperor Theodosius whose residence was in Constantinople and Eugenius, his opponent from pagan Rome. This battle was of world historical significance. Across this territory the Visigoths invaded Italy at the beginning of the 5th century and conquered Rome. In the middle of the century they were followed by the

Huns who razed Aquileia, and at the end of the century by the Ostrogoths. In 489 their king Theodoric the Great, an ally of the Eastern Roman Emperor, defeated the Roman usurper, the Germanic army leader Odoacer, near the Soča River. The Ostrogoths subsequently became rulers of Italy, became Romanized very quickly, and for over half a century ruled over the territory of present-day Slovenia.

In the middle of the 6th century the Lombards, a Germanic tribe from the Pannonian Plain, came to the territory of Slovenia. Archeological finds, the most important being those from graves at Kranj, are proof of their short stay in Slovenia. Tradition has it that the Lombards left Slovenia at Easter in 568, setting out for Italy where they destroyed the Byzantine authority which had been established there in the meantime, and although few in number created a powerful state.

2. The Ethnic Dominance of the Slavs and Their State of Karantanija

After the departure of the Lombards, a Slavic people, the ancestors of the present-day Slovenes, dominated the territory of present-day Slovenia and much farther north, as far as the south bank of the Danube. It is not known precisely from where or exactly when they appeared in this region, and historians offer several hypotheses regarding their origin and settlement here.

According to the first hypothesis, a Slavic people settled here in the time of the migration of nations after the year 500, coming from the area of the West Slavs, and at the end of the 6th century another wave of Slavs arrived in this region from the southeast by following the Sava and Drava rivers as far as their sources.

A second hypothesis which is slowly losing ground speaks only of the settling of this region by Slavs from the Slav southeast.

Recently a hypothesis has appeared supported only by some amateur historians according to which the Slavs are presumed to have settled this region from the first millennium B.C. and that the Veneti are the direct ancestors of the Slav ethnos that dominated here at the end of the 6th century. So far this hypothesis has been insufficiently investigated scientifically.

Existing sources only bear witness to the fact that between 580 and 590 the Slavs conquered some late Roman towns in this region, the former Noricum, and as allies of the nomadic Turko-Mongolian Avars defeated the Bavarians near Agunt (near Lienz in eastern Tyrol) in 595. Conflict with the Bavarians continued for nearly three centuries, and the first boundary between them was fixed so that the Slavs occupied a part of the Eastern Alps. From the beginning of the 7th century, the Slavs settled southward into northern Istria and to the outermost eastern hilly margin of Italy as far as Cividale, a stronghold of the local Lombard dukes.

About the social organization that developed in this region, which in Latin sources from the neighbouring Germanic Lombard and Bavarian states from the beginning of the 7th century was referred to as the Slav province, we have little reliable information. Some rare sources say that until 626 the nomadic Avar horsemen ruled over a Slav serf population in this region. Numerous other sources and more serious investigations speak of the independent life of the Slavs here and of their tribal organization, but as a community they were subordinate to the military and political ruling role of the Avars. Their mutual relations were the relations of military alliance and of Avar incursions into the region, as there were few permanent Avar settlements in Karantanija and the area along the Sava River. At the beginning of the 7th century, the Slavs together with the Avars invaded eastern parts of the Lombard State and besieged Cividale.

Through contact with the Lombard and the Bavarian society, the Slav society developed in a Slav province called Karantanija. In this tribal society a new social class with special moral and political status began to develop, the *Kosezi* or military escort of the highest prince. While this class did not enjoy any economic privileges, it was a pillar of princely authority and of a kind of Slav protostate. This state grew from the revolt of the Slavs between 626 and 630 against Avar authority which only a short time earlier had been considerably weakened by the Avar defeat before Byzantium. This Slav state of Karantanija in the area of the present-day Austrian province of Carinthia that possibly included the present-day Styria-Drau Region is the first Slav state mentioned in written sources. These sources testify to its links with the great Kingdom of Samo in Bohemia and Moravia in the middle of the 7th century. Until the 13th century the name "*Karantanci*" for the inhabitants of Karantanija was the first to be found in written documents for the present-day Slovenes. The Karantanci, who in their predominantly tribal society were free members of village communities and represented the majority along with the serfs originating from the captured Romanic Christian natives, elected their dukes at a special ceremony at the Duke's Stone at Krn Castle which was the center of the state. Before all the assembled free people, the duke had to swear that he would respect and defend the people's will and their rights. Only then did the peasant or "*kosez*" sitting on the Duke's Stone, the capital of an Ionic column from ancient Virunum which had stood in the vicinity of Krn Castle, relinquish his seat, for which the duke gave him a horse and a speckled bull in return. Nowhere else in Europe was such a ceremony then known. The ceremony was preserved into the late Middle Ages long after the Slavs had lost their political independence and the feudal Duchy of Carinthia was ruled by the German aristocracy. At that time the ceremony of the enthronement of the provincial duke was conducted in a Slav language and was so interesting that it was recorded by numerous chroniclers between the 12th and 14th centuries.

Some of these medieval chronicles were known to the French lawyer and philosopher Jean Bodin in the 16th century, and he described this Carinthian ceremony in his legal work as a democratic act of inaugurating a ruler. The work of Jean Bodin drew the attention of the American lawyer and politician Thomas Jefferson, Father of the American Constitution and third President of the United States.

The state of Karantanija survived as an independent entity until the middle of the 8th century. There are some indications that in this period the Slavs south of Karantanija, that is, south of the Karavanke Mountains in the Sava River watershed, also had their own principality, called Carniola by the Lombard chroniclers.

3. The Fall of Independent Karantanija

Around the year 740, Avar attacks on Karantanija increased considerably. Karantanija felt itself too weak to resist the Avars and requested help from the Bavarians. The Bavarians sent help and defended Karantanija but demanded that it recognize Bavarian supremacy. This was agreed in 745, and as a guarantee of their vassal loyalty, the Karantanci had to send prominent members of their royal family as hostages to Bavaria.

In the second half of the 8th century Christianity began to spread from Bavaria to Karantanija. For their missionary work among the Karantanci, the Bavarians established two important missionary outposts at Innichen in present-day East Tyrol and at Kremsmunster in Upper Austria. These two outposts reflect how far the Slav tribes had settled by the 8th century. The first to convert to Christianity were Karantanija's royal hostages Gorazd and Hotimir who spread Christianity following their return to the throne of Karantanija. Primarily serving this purpose were Irish missionaries from Salzburg. Part of the population of Karantanija resisted Christianization, but the Karantanija vassal prince Valtunk crushed the major anti-Christian revolt with Bavarian help. When the Bavarian state eventually submitted to the Franks in 788, the vassal but internally still independent Slav Karantanija also fell under Frankish domination but maintained its internal independence for several more decades. Most probably the Karantanci and Carniolans collaborated in the Frankish military expeditions against the Avars between 794 and 796 that finally destroyed the Avar military force and the Avar people in general.

Between 819 and 823, Slavs from Carniola (the upper Sava region) and Karantanija joined the uprising centered in Sisak of Ljudevit Posavski against Frankish rule. When after several military expeditions the Franks crushed the revolt, they closely incorporated the Slav vassal principalities of Karantanija and Carniola into their own social and political system. They abolished their internal autonomy, deposed the local princes, and subjected both provinces to the margrave of their eastern prefecture centered somewhere in present-day Austria. Thus both principalities were joined to Western European civilization. The Frankish feudal system began to spread throughout the region, and the Frankish feudal aristocracy began arriving, granted lands by the Frankish ruler. The representatives of the Slav upper class that was just beginning to arise in the former principalities of Karantanija and Carniola were engulfed by the Frankish feudal class. Thus the Slav population living there lost its upper social classes. However, the mass of primarily Slav rural serf population managed to maintain its identity, which was different from the Germanic

Bavarian-Frankish identity, through its language. For long centuries it was this Slav language that became the specific difference that distinguished the population of this province (later called Slovenia) from the Germanic (later German) populations in the neighbouring provinces of the common state called the Holy Roman Empire after 962. For its needs among the Slav inhabitants of Karantanija and Carniola, the Catholic Church recorded certain prayers in the Slovene language. A text, though not the original, has been preserved from around the year 1000 and presents prayer forms used in the Frankish state in the time of Charlemagne.

The attempt to get the Slav population its own church in its own language, which would differ from the Latin Frankish Church, was merely an episode lasting only a few years. Between 867 and 873, the Slav prince Kocelj, who ruled in Blatenski Kostel in Pannonia in the western part of Hungary, invited to his territory the two missionaries Cyril and Methodius who had previously been spreading the Christian faith in the Slav language in the neighbouring Slav state of Greater Moravia. They were Greek by birth but knew the language of the Macedonian Slavs and had been sent to Greater Moravia by the Byzantine Emperor at the request of its prince who was fighting against the Franks. In 869 they left Kocelj's Pannonia for Rome and from Pope Nicholas II (867-872) received permission to spread Christianity using the Pannonian Slav language and its new Glagolitic alphabet. Cyril died in Rome in 869, while his brother Methodius was appointed Bishop of Pannonia and Moravia. Until the end of his reign sometime around 873 or 874, Prince

Kocelj decisively supported the Slav liturgy of Methodius and his disciples in the face of strong opposition from the Latin-Frankish Catholic Church in Salzburg. Around the year 874 Kocelj disappeared from politics, the Franks annexed his country to the Eastern March that also included Karantanija, and under pressure from the Salzburg Church Methodius and his disciples had to leave Pannonia. Temporarily they went to Greater Moravia and at the end of the 9th century to the Croatian state and on to the Macedonian Slavs. After that the Salzburg Church again completely dominated Lower Pannonia and removed every trace of the Slav liturgy. All these events are described in the famous Salzburg record *Conversio Bagoariorum et Carantanorum*. The Hungarian invasion of Pannonia drove out Frankish authority and threatened the whole Eastern March, including Karantanija and Carniola. The Germanic-German counteroffensive that from 955 (the Battle of Lechfeld near Augsburg) greatly weakened the Hungarians and drove them from the Eastern March secured the region for German colonization, thus cutting off Slav peoples south of the Danube from the Slavs of Bohemia and Moravia. The Slavs in Karantanija and Carniola were left to their own development that in the following centuries led to the formation of the Slovenes and Slovenia.

4. The Political Division of Slovene Territory in the Middle Ages

The renewed Germanic-German authority over the Slav territory after the victory over the Hungarians fortified itself by creating frontier marches that included and divided the original Slav territory. Roughly from north to south these marches were Carinthia, the Karantanija March (present-day Central Styria), the Drava Basin or Ptuj March, the Savinja March that spread south across the Sava River as far as Višnja gora in Dolenjska, the Sava Basin March in the Upper Sava Basin, and the Istrian March. These marches strengthened the borders of the Holy Roman Empire against Hungary and Croatia, and thus the eastern ethnic boundary between the Slovenes and the Hungarians and Croats was formed. This boundary has remained essentially the same for a thousand years.

In the course of development in the High Middle Ages, the ruling feudal lords – margraves, dukes, and others – transformed these marches into their own dynastic territories that developed into historical provinces within the framework of the Holy Roman Empire. A Slovene population wholly or partly dominated these provinces or parts of them. Around the year 1000 the Duchy of Carinthia was politically the most important province. It had been raised to a duchy in 976 because Emperor Otto II wanted to weaken the overly powerful tribal Duchy of Bavaria. With the Duchy of Carinthia as their center, all the eastern marches – the Karantanija March, the Drava, Savinja, Sava Basin, and Istrian Marches, and even the Friuli and Verona Marches – were then linked for some time, giving Greater Carinthia immense political and strategic importance. From the middle of the 11th century, individual marches and their ruling feudal lords gradually became increasingly independent and through battles with one another, marriages, and dynastic contracts rounded off their territories and changed the borders of their marches to form the historical provinces.

The first to escape the authority of the Carinthian dukes were the Verona and Friuli marches. In the Friuli March, the Patriarch of Aquileia acquired strong secular power and in the course of time also became its formal secular prince. In other Slovene marches and lands as well, the rulers granted large estates to the Church, in particular to the Salzburg Diocese, the Freising Diocese (the Škofja Loka dominion), and the Brixen Diocese (the Bled dominion) in the Sava Basin or Carniola March, as it was called after the year 1000. The church property of these three dioceses and several smaller church territories did not develop into independent provinces, but with their rights of political immunity they represented an important political factor in strengthening or limiting the authority of the provincial rulers.

From the second part of the 11th century, the Counts of Waimar-Orlamünde governed the Carniola March and also had authority over Istria. When their line died out, their authority passed to the Counts of Andechs who adopted the name Meran after their possessions in Rijeka and Istria (then Meranija). Kamnik became their family seat.

In the middle of the 11th century the Karantanija March began to become independent of Greater Carinthia, and the name Styria (Štajerska) after the town of Stayr where its margraves the Traungaus originated soon came into common use. The Traungaus gradually spread their authority southward into the Drava Basin March (1147) and also acquired significant property in the Savinja March (the Laško dominion), thus reaching the Sava River. Under the last Traungau count, Ottokar IV, Styria was raised to a duchy in 1180.

The Savinja March lost its Counts of Krajišnik dynasty relatively early (in the middle of the 11th century) and did not form into an independent province. Parts of this march south of the Sava River (the Višnja gora dominion) had already been appropriated by the Andechs-Meran dynasty of Carniola, who incorporated them in the newly forming province of Carniola.

At the beginning of the 13th century, the two strongest dynasties in Slovene territory were the Spanheims of Carinthia and the Bambergs of Styria. In 1228 the Spanheims inherited the property and titles of the extinct Andechs-Meran dynasty in Carniola and also conquered territory in the Krka River basin (Krško polje) as far as the Gorjanci mountain range where they established the Cistercian monastery at Kostanjevica beside the Krka River. After the death of the last Traungau in 1192, the Austrian ducal Bamberg dynasty asserted itself in Styria and tried to strengthen its authority as far as the Sava River where in 1208 it built a bridge over the Savinja River at its confluence with the Sava (Zidani most). At the same time, the Patriarch of Aquileia was asserting himself as the secular ruler in Istria, while in the territory where he originally held authority, the Friuli March, the Counts of Gorizia were attaining independence and forming a special political and administrative unit.

The second half of the 13th century was an important turning point in the political development of the Slovene provinces. One after another the two most important feudal dynasties died out: the Bambergs in 1246 and the Spanheims in 1269. Within a little over two decades, the Bohemian King Ottokar Premysl II had seized the property of both dynasties. At the beginning of the 1270's, his rule extended from the Krkonoše Mountains to the Adriatic Sea and also included Austria.

However, as early as 1273 the power and possessions of the great Ottokar were threatened. The new Hapsburg emperor of the Holy Roman (German) Empire, Rudolf I, revoked all of Ottokar acquisitions made during the Great Interregnum because they were imperial feuds and as such could be only granted by the duly elected Holy Roman (German) Emperor. These acquisitions included Austria, Styria, Carinthia, Carniola, Istria, and even Friuli where Ottokar's rule reached. Ottokar refused to return these provinces and war erupted with the Emperor who was supported by several German princes who feared the overly powerful Ottokar. In 1278 Ottokar lost the battle and his life near Dürnkrut on the plains of Moravia. Emperor Rudolf at once awarded the imperial feuds of Austria and Styria to his sons, while Carinthia and Carniola temporarily fell to the Mainhard dynasty of Tyrol and Gorizia. When this dynasty died out in 1335, all their lands with the exception of the County of Gorizia were seized by the Hapsburgs who immediately raised Carniola to a duchy.

In 1374 the Hapsburgs inherited properties in the Slovene March (eastern Dolenjska), in

Metlika (Bela Krajina), and in Istria (the County of Pazin) from one of the Counts of Gorizia. In fear of Venice, the city of Trieste and its hinterland resorted to the protection of the Hapsburgs in 1382. By the second half of the 14th century, the Hapsburgs ruled nearly all the Slovene territory. Outside their authority remained only the County of Gorizia and the western Istrian towns with their hinterland where the Venetian Republic imposed its authority between 1267 and 1284 and maintained it until its fall in 1797. In the territory of the Venetian Republic a different style of culture developed than in continental Slovenia, the Venetian-Mediterranean culture which also influenced the otherwise Hapsburg Trieste.

In their provinces the Hapsburgs immediately subjugated all the ancient allodial and ministerial nobility and towns. All swore allegiance to the Hapsburgs.

Only at the beginning of the 15th century did the Hapsburgs acquire a political rival in Slovene territory, the dynasty of the Counts of Celje. This family originated from the Žovnek Castle in the Savinja Valley (they were titled after the castle for half a century) where their allodial possession is proven in written documents from as early as 1130. Over the following two centuries they spread and strengthened their possessions and their renown as lawyers for several Church properties. In 1308 the Žovneks surrendered their allodial possessions to the Hapsburgs, immediately receiving them back as a feud. In 1333 the Žovneks acquired through marriage the property of the Counts of Vovberg (based in Carinthia) with a powerful castle at Celje to which they transferred their seat from Žovnek. In 1341 Emperor Ludwig IV of Bavaria raised them to nobility and bestowed upon them the title of Counts of Celje. Their coat-of-arms has three six-point stars on a blue background. In the shape of their coat-of-arms some see a stylized Holy Grail, which was supposedly hidden at Rogatec in the territory of Slovenia. The glorious rise of the Counts of Celje began at the end of the 14th century when the Celje dynasty was ruled by Count Herman II. He conducted a skillful dynastic policy and made alliances with distinguished European feudal houses. The most important was his alliance and friendship with Emperor Sigismund of Luxembourg whom Count Herman supposedly saved from drowning in the Danube after the battle with the Turks near Nikopolje in 1396. Sigismund afterwards married Herman's daughter Barbara of Celje. In the following years the Emperor bestowed rich gifts of property upon the Counts of Celje and gave them important posts in the Slovene provinces and in Croatia. The Counts of Celje also had family ties through Herman's son Friderik with the Frankopans, one of Croatia's most powerful feudal families.

In 1418 fortune once again smiled on the Counts of Celje. They inherited the property of the Ortenburgs, one of the mightiest feudal families in Carinthia and Carniola. They thus received large possessions around Spittal in Carinthia, and in Carniola they acquired the domains of Radovljica and Kočevje which they colonized in the second half of the 14th century with settlers from their German properties in Upper Carinthia.

In 1423, as a result of pressure from the Emperor, the Hapsburgs had to waive their feudal authority over the Counts of Celje who thus became direct counts of the Holy Roman Empire. In 1436 Emperor Sigismund raise the Counts of Celje to the rank of imperial princes and their Celje and Ortenburg possessions to the rank of principalities, direct imperial feuds. The Counts of Celje rapidly began to give the principality of Celje all the characteristics of an independent princely state. They founded a court of justice for the princely nobility, and there are some indications that they were endeavouring to found their own diocese at Celje. The last Count of Celje, Prince Ulrich II or Urh, conducted an ambitious foreign policy of extensive Central European and Balkan links and married a daughter of the Serbian despot Jurij Branković. For his relative Ladislav Posthumus he was also King's regent in Hungary, a fact the Hungarian nobility resented. In 1456 their representative János Hunyadi killed him in Belgrade where Ulrich II had come to organize the defence of the city against the Turks.

After the death of Ulrich II, the last Count of Celje, the Hapsburgs again acquired the possessions of the Counts of Celje after a brief war with Jan Vitovec, the commander-in-chief of the Celje widow Katarina. The development of the special principality of Celje, this short-lived state centered in Slovene territory, thus came to a close.

5. Social, Economic, and Cultural Development in Slovenia during the Middle Ages

After the authority of the German Holy Roman Empire over Slovenia was again strengthened after the victory over the Hungarians

(955), the process of feudalization accelerated. The German Holy Roman Emperor, the nominal supreme owner of all uncultivated land, distributed this land to various feudal lords from margraves to lesser feudal nobles and also accepted the feudal subjection of all the great landowners of the time who thus entered the ranks of the feudal aristocracy. When free peasants, members of village communities, set out to till previously uncultivated land in their immediate neighbourhood, as was necessary every few years according to their method of cultivation, they had to acknowledge the ownership and authority of the landlord and thus gradually fell into feudal servitude.

In the 11th century, the plough and three-year crop rotation made their influence felt on agriculture in Slovenia, giving the possibility of employment to a greater number of people.

The dominant form of property ownership and production in Slovene territory was not one in which the feudal lords themselves were involved in the cultivation of land, although some were, but rather there were subject farms called "*hubas*" that were joined in farming settlements or villages. One reason for this was the social and economic structure established before feudalism asserted itself: it was a free rural community in the time when there were no serf-owning latifundia in the territory that could simply be converted into feudal estates. Secondly, the predominantly hilly Slovene landscape did not provide conditions for the development of that type of economy. Furthermore, the social and political thinking that came from developed feudal countries was undoubtedly decisive, namely that a farmer on his own farm worked better and produced more than a farm hand on a feudal estate.

As in the more developed feudal countries, the feudal nobility built fortified residences or castles on their estates in Slovenia that to a large extent controlled the whole territory by the first half of the 13th century. Emperors, margraves, and dukes presented numerous extensive properties to the Church, that is, to dioceses that had their seats outside Slovene territory. Thus, the Archdiocese of Salzburg became the greatest landowner with properties in Carinthia, in Styria (Ptuj), and in nearly the whole Sava region from Sevnica to Brežice. Salzburg had acquired a great deal of its property even before the Hungarian invasions at the end of the 9th century, and some later as well. In 973, a large estate in the vicinity of Škofja Loka was given to the Bavarian diocese of Freising, and in 1004 the Brixen diocese in Tyrol acquired a large estate stretching from Bled to Bohinj. The Frankish diocese of Bamberg acquired property around present-day Villach and in the center of their property built the town where an important trade route crossed the Drau River. In 1001 the Patriarch of Aquileia acquired large properties on the Soča River including Solkan Castle and the village of Gorizia and in 1040 another large estate in the Carniola March between Cerknica and Lož. In the following centuries other dioceses including the Gurk and Lavant dioceses acquired estates on Slovene territory.

Throughout the Middle Ages from Charlemagne in 803 until the church reforms of Emperor Joseph II, Slovene territory was divided in the canonical sense into two archdioceses, the Salzburg Archdiocese and the Patriarchate of Aquileia. The border between the two ran along the Drava River.

In the 11th century, eight Benedictine monasteries (two women's and six men's) came into being in Carinthia, then predominantly Slovene ethnic territory, among them those at Ossiach, Millstatt, St. Paul, and Arnoldstein. The first monastery founded in the territory of present-day Slovenia was the Cistercian monastery at Stična founded by Patriarch Peregrin of Aquileia and the feudal lord Friderik of Višnja gora. These monasteries played an important role in the colonization of the surrounding territory and in introducing more prudent farming methods such as the system of three-year crop rotation and the production of cheese and smoked meat.

The feudal lords were interested in increasing the number of farmers on their estates in order to obtain greater income and power. They therefore introduced the colonization of their estates, that is, the cultivation of untilled land on which they settled mainly the surplus population from their existing *hubas* in Slovene territory and from their German estates as well. In the process of this agrarian colonization during the high and late Middle Ages, the ethnic border of this territory that at the end of the 6th century had been predominantly settled by Slavs changed fundamentally. By the end of the Middle Ages, the border between the German and the Slav-Slovene population ran through the middle of Carinthia, through the center of the Klagenfurt Basin from the southern foothills of the Koralpe and Saualpe mountains in the east across Maria

Saal north of Klagenfurt to Ossiacher See and from there to Villach and then along the northern margin of the Gail Valley as far as Hermagor in the west. This border was preserved with minimal changes until the end of the 19th century.

From the beginning of the 12th century, towns and boroughs began to develop in the interior of Slovene territory. In Slovene Primorska, coastal towns such as Trieste, Koper, Izola, and Piran had existed continually from antiquity. These new towns in particular were the harbingers and bearers of a new economy (more highly developed crafts and trade) and a new social class of townspeople that differed distinctly from both the rural feudal serf class and the feudal nobility. A predominantly free population lived in the towns and by their autonomy were separate from the agrarian feudal environment and subject only to their town lords, either the provincial prince himself, a major feudal lord, or a Church noble (e.g., Breže, Villach, Klagenfurt, Maribor, Ptuj, Sevnica, Rajhenburg, Ljubljana, Kranj, and Kamnik). The towns in the interior developed according to the model of southern German towns, and these assumed the latter's social and political organization.

Until the high Middle Ages the power in Primorska towns was in the hands of the townspeople or the bishop. At the end of the 13th century, however, all these towns together with their agrarian hinterlands, with the exception of Trieste, fell under the authority of the Venetian Republic and were ruled according to the Venetian model by a town council to which only the higher class of citizens, the patricians, could be elected. In the area of Primorska towns and their agrarian hinterlands, a type of Mediterranean Venetian civilization therefore developed.

Throughout the Middle Ages Slovenia thus developed culturally under the influence of two cultural centers: the dominant southern German influence and the Aquileian-Venetian influence. On Slovene territory a considerable number of buildings of ecclesiastic and secular character were built in the Romanesque style that have survived on the coast as well as in the interior until the present. Among the most beautiful are the castles in Breže, Ptuj, Podsreda, and Kamnik and the churches in Gurk, Millstatt, Stična, Trieste, Koper, and elsewhere. Many were later renovated in the Gothic and baroque styles (Laško, Loka). Many more Gothic buildings have been preserved: Bled Castle, the lower Celje Castle, Ormož Castle, etc., and the Gothic churches on Ptujska gora and Svetina as well as numerous town parish churches and monastery churches such as those in Škofja Loka, Radovljica, Kranj, Viktring, Ptuj, Lenart, Novo mesto, Kostanjevica, Pleterje, Žiče, and Piran. A special form of Gothic architecture are the small Gothic country churches, beautifully decorated with frescoes, found from Primorska to Prekmurje: Hrastovlje, Suha pri Škofji Loki, Črn grob, Sv. Janez on Lake Bohinj, Mače nad Preddvorom, Sv. Primož nad Kamnikom, etc.

In several monasteries (Viktring, Stična, Žiče) there were renowned manuscript schools where many eminent documents important in Slovene history originated. People from Slovene territory rose to become important European scientists. One such person was Herman of

Carinthia in the 13th century, who among other things studied Arabian writers. Extensive trade flowed across Slovene territory between the Austrian, Bohemian, and Hungarian provinces and Italy bringing economic, social, political, and cultural views to Slovenia.

Until the beginning of the 15th century, a uniform serf class on one hand and a class of feudal landlords on the other eventually formed within the framework of the feudal order in Slovene territory. In the middle of the 15th century Turkish raids into Slovene lands intensified and had dire consequences in the lives of the population who were pillaged, murdered, and taken into slavery by these "Turkish" (in fact, Southern Slav-Balkan) raiders. Initially, the rural population had no protection as the provincial prince and authorities were slow to organize defenses. The organization of defence was the reason the provincial prince Friderik of Hapsburg introduced direct provincial taxes on the serfs which provoked widespread revolt among the rural population as well as a great crisis in the feudal system.

The Turkish raids and the need for defences against them caused ordinary rural people to build their own fortifications, the anti-Turkish *tabors* or encampments. Most often they built a strong wall with defensive towers around churches on hills where they could defend themselves against the mounted Turkish marauders. These *tabors*, many of which have survived to the present, are a specialty of Slovene architecture in all of Slovene territory.

II. THE BIRTH OF THE SLOVENE NATION

6. Peasant Uprisings, Humanism, and Reformation

In Slovene territory the period from the end of the 15th to the end of the 16th century was a period of great peasant uprisings, defence against the Turks, and the development of new towns, a time of Humanism and the Protestant Reformation that was of decisive importance for the development of the Slovene nation.

There were numerous reasons for the peasant uprising including the introduction of new direct taxes by the provincial prince, the transformation of the old feudal tax system into new less favourable forms (e.g., the introduction of socage service) that thwarted any possibility for the peasant to improve his position, and dissatisfaction with the poor defence under which the rural population suffered the most.

The first to resist were the peasants in Carinthia who between 1473 and 1476 united in a peasant union called the *Bund*. In Slovene this word became "*punt*" meaning "revolt." The *punt* had its center in the Drau Valley, and by the spring of 1478 it embraced nearly all of Slovene territory as well as a part of German Carinthia. In some places towns-people and miners (Villach-Villach, Huttenberg) sympathized with the peasant "*puntarji*" (rebels). The *puntarji* refused to pay taxes to their feudal lords and began to collect taxes themselves and demanded the right to decide themselves on provincial taxes to their prince. They also began to elect their own judges. "With these moves, the demands and actions of rural self-confidence outgrew the possibilities provided by the existing social framework" (V. Simoniti).

The Emperor forbade extraordinary gatherings of peasants and ordered the uprising suppressed. However, before the army of noblemen could set out, the Turks poured into Carinthia in the summer of 1478, slaughtering a peasant army of around six hundred men near Coccau in the Val Canale valley (Italy) and then ravaging the countryside.

At the beginning of the 16th century, Emperor Maximilian of Hapsburg became involved in a war with the Venetian Republic on the very edge of Slovene territory. The needs of the army only intensified the tax pressure. In addition to the new taxes, the peasants also suffered because of the loss of trade with Italy, particularly the loss of income from freightage between Hungary and Italy.

In the first months of 1515, the large union of peasants that we call the Pan-Slovene uprising developed in Carniola and spread into Styria and the karst region. This peasant union sent a delegation to Emperor Maximilian in Augsburg to demand the abolishment of the newly introduced taxes and the restoration of the previous conditions (their "ancient rights"). The Emperor promised only a fair investigation and demanded that the peasant union be dissolved. The peasants did not obey and even more joined the revolt. It is estimated that at the height of the uprising in the spring of 1515, about 80,000 subjects were involved. Dissatisfaction grew into open resistance, and the rebels attacked and burned castles, in some places even killing their landlords. The nobility retreated to the towns. The rebels reached the height of their success in May and June. The nobility pleaded with the Emperor for help, and in the middle of June he sent an army of mercenaries that together with the army of the provincial nobility under the leadership of Jurij of Herberstein, the joint commander of the Inner Austrian provinces, routed the rebels at Konjice and Celje. After the army entered Carniola near Brežice, the rebellion was soon suppressed. The weakne-sses of the rebels were their poor communications, lack of mobility, and, of course, their military inexperience and inadequate weaponry. The nobility took cruel revenge: in Graz alone, 161 rebels were put to death, and a special tax, the *puntarski pfenig* ("rebel pfennig"), was imposed upon the peasantry.

From this Slovene peasant uprising the first printed Slovene words are preserved in a German leaflet, the slogan of the rebels: "*Stara pravda*" ("The Ancient Rights") and "*Leukup, leukup, leukup uboga gmaina*" ("Let us unite, poor common people").

In the second half of the 16th century there was a great Slovene-Croatian peasant uprising in the eastern parts of Slovene Styria, Carniola, and the neighbouring Croatian regions of Zagorje and Posavina. The rebellion erupted at the beginning of 1573 on the Zagorje estates of Stubica and Susedgrad belonging to Baron Ferenc Tahy, who was hated by the farmers for his brutality. This time the peasants were better organized since some of the Croatian peasants and yeomen had military experience from battles against the Turks in the border marches. In addition to the traditional peasant demands, the rebels this time manifested a very self-confident and ambitious political program. They demanded the removal of the feudal lords as an unnecessary and parasitic social class, the establishment of an imperial regency in Zagreb, the takeover of care of the border, and exemption from tolls and duties for agricultural trade. The Croatian parliament sent an army of nobles and *uskoki* (mercenary soldiers from Serbia and Bosnia who had fled before the Turks and were later settled along the border as a line of defense) from the March against the rebels. There were numerous skirmishes and defeats of smaller peasant detachments, including in Slovenia near Krško and at Sv. Peter pod Sv. Gorami on the Sotla River. The main battle between some 12,000 rebels and the parliamentary army occurred at the beginning of February near Stubiške toplice, and the rebels were utterly defeated. Three thousand are supposed to have lost their lives, and many were later victims of the nobility's revenge.

Peasant uprisings continued in Slovene territory with greater or lesser intensity until the abolition of feudalism 250 years later.

In the second half of the 15th and at the beginning of the 16th century, the lively flow of trade and people across Slovene territory also brought Renaissance and Humanist ideas. People from Slovene regions (here it is not possible to distinguish people according to their ethnic origin) studied at the University of Vienna and at German and Italian universities. According to historically recognized sources, their numbers were considerable. Many adopted

Renaissance and Humanist views and represented them in their work and functions. Some of these rose to prominent positions in the Hapsburg lands, for example, Tomaž Prelokar from Celje (Thomas de Cilia), who was a professor at the University of Vienna and the first Humanist teacher of the future Emperor Maximilian. He finished his rise in the prominent Bishop's seat in Constance. Also from Celje was Brikcij Preprost, a professor and several times dean at the Faculty of Arts of the University of Vienna and twice its rector.

Nearby Laško was the home of the many-sided Avguštin Prygl (called *Tyfernus* after his birthplace). He was the first collector of antique inscriptions in Slovene territory and in the wider Central European area. As an architect he was active in Ljubljana, building a new bishop's manor in 1520 for his schoolmate and friend, the eminent Humanist Bishop Krištof Ravbar. He also built a bishop's manor for Bishop Slatkonja in Vienna. From Zgornja Ščavnica in Styria (Štajerska) came the dean, rector, and superintendent of the University of Vienna Bernard Perper who wrote the first Humanist Latin grammar, reprinted numerous times in the last two decades of the 15th century. From Vače in Carniola came Matija Hvale, a professor and philosopher who strove for a Humanist reform of philosophy studies at the university and the first Slovene to write a philosophical work of nominalistic orientation.

The eminent Hapsburg diplomat Žiga (Sigismund) Herberstein (1486-1562) was a native of Vipava but lived mostly in Vienna or was on diplomatic postings. Among other places he served in Moscow, the basis for his essay *Rerum Moscaviticarum comentarii* ("The Moscow Records") that was published in 1549 and reprinted in several European countries and languages.

Of course, we should not leave out two important Church dignitaries who were also zealous humanists. The first is the Bishop of Ljubljana Sigismund Lamberg (1461-1488) who studied in Padua and later sent nearly all the leading clergy of his diocese to study at Italian Humanist universities. He successor Bishop Ravbar also studied there.

The second is the Bishop of Trieste Petro Bonomo (1502-1546) who was well acquainted with Humanism and deeply committed to it and who viewed the Reformation with sympathy. He was in the service of the Vienna court for many years. Upon his return to Trieste he transformed the Bishop's Court into the leading Humanist and Reformation center in Slovene territory. The leading Slovene Protestant Primož Trubar adopted Humanist and Reformation ideas from him.

The first appearance of the Reformation with its radical heresies and Lutheran orientation was evident in Slovene regions at the end of the 1520's. Sources bear witness to Reformist circles in Carinthia in Slovenj Gradec and Radgona, as well as in Carniola in the surroundings of Kamnik and in Ljubljana. In Ljubljana one such Protestant circle was headed from 1529 by the secretary of the provincial council Matija Klombner. The circle included other distinguished citizens as well as a number of priests. Through Primož Trubar the circle was also linked with the Trieste circle of Bishop Petro Bonomo.

Primož Trubar was born in Rašica in Dolenjska in 1508, the son of a serf of the Count of Turjak (Auersperg). As a bright young man he studied in Rijeka, Vienna, and Trieste where he received excellent Humanist and theological training and became familiar with the doctrines of Luther, Zwingli, Pellicon, and Bullinger. In 1530 he was ordained as a priest by Bishop Bonomo and sent as a vicar to the parish of Laško that extended as far as Loka near Zidani most. Here he was already discreetly proclaiming Protestant religious views and speaking rationally against superstition. In 1535 he left to be a preacher in Ljubljana but after five years had to retreat to Trieste under pressure from opponents of the Reformation. He again worked in Ljubljana for several years among the Protestants who were spreading the Protestant religion and books in the German language, the only appropriate language as it was used by all educated people in Slovene territories, regardless of German or Slovene ethnic origin. In 1548 the Hapsburgs intensified their pressure against the Protestants in their hereditary lands, and Trubar was forced to go into exile to Protestant areas in Germany. He embraced Lutheranism and worked as pastor in Nürnberg, Rothenburg, Kempten, Urach, Tübingen, and Derendingen.

His Humanist and religious conviction that every Christian should read the *Bible* himself had highly significant cultural and historical consequences for the people of the country of his origin. He decided to acquaint his people, the "*Lubim Slovencem*" or "Dear Slovenes" as he was the first person in history to address them, with the text of the *Bible* in their own language, which until then had not developed as a literary language. In 1550 he therefore had to first write two basic books, an elementary grammar book and a catechism. With this epochal work Trubar entered history as "the Father of Slovene Nation." The Slovene nation was thus metaphorically speaking "born from the Word," as John the Evangelist says of the creation of the world.

As the basis for the Slovene literary language, Trubar chose the speech of his birthplace Rašica. Because it was the dialect of the central part of Slovene territory, it was a well-chosen standard which "every good simple Slovene could easily understand." It was clear to Trubar that such Slovene was spoken not only in Carniola but also in Lower Styria, Carinthia, Trieste, and Gorizia. In addition to his grammar book and catechism, Trubar also wrote a number of other books necessary for the liturgy and school use in Slovene territory. Let us mention only his translation of the *New Testament* on which he worked for twenty-two years (from 1555-1577) and the *Cerkovna ordninga* of 1564.

In 1561, following a summons from the largely Protestant Carniola Provincial Council, Trubar returned to Carniola for four years and became superintendent of the Protestant Church. In this time he wrote the *Cerkovna ordninga* for "the Church of this Slovene language," demonstrating that he was aware of his duty and had ambitions that his Protestant Lutheran Würtemberg Church Organization, which was only recognized in Carniola, spread throughout the whole of Slovene ethnic territory. In his *Cerkovna ordninga* Trubar also outlined the organization of primary schools: in every parish there should be an educated person, preferably the parish priest, who would teach children to read and write in the Slovene language. Beside Trubar stood numerous Protestant Slovenes, some very highly educated, who also wrote and translated many important books, thus raising Slovenes to their place in the circle of developed and cultured European nations. The scholar Adam Bohorič wrote *Arctice horule*, a grammar of the Slovene language in Latin, praising in his introduction the Slovene language as a member of the great Slavic family of languages. Jurij Dalmatin from the Sava region went to Würtemberg where increasing numbers of Slovene Protestants lived after 1565 and translated the entire *Bible* which was published in 1584. His translation consolidated Slovene literary standards and proved that the Slovene language was mature enough to cope with the highest works of art. Regarding all the actions of the Slovene Protestants, it is important to note that they were politically and materially supported by a great number of citizens as well as by many nobleman, proving that at the time people were not as horizontally divided according to their ethnic origin as Slovene history and literary history stated at the beginning of the 20th century.

In the Protestant period, the printing house of Janž Mandelc in Ljubljana published several books, but the majority of books were printed in Germany. The cultural activities of the Slovene

Protestants must be considered the cultural birth of the Slovene nation. Through their views and work they created a clear and far-sighted concept of the Slovene people and their cultural perspective that was raised again by the Enlightenment two hundred years later after the period of political pressure of absolutism and the Counter Reformation.

7. The Counter Reformation and the Rise of Absolutism

After the death in 1590 of Inner Austria's Archduke Karl of Hapsburg, who had compromised with the Protestant provincial councils and allowed them the freedom of Protestant faith, his son Ferdinand began his rule of the Inner Austrian provinces (Styria, Carinthia, Carniola, Gorizia, Trieste, and Istria). An ardent Catholic, he was educated at the Jesuit college in Graz, which by 1586 had developed into a university. Within a few years, the course of events had turned so that he could begin an extensive anti-Protestant campaign that had far-reaching consequences for Slovene regions and Slovene national and cultural development.

In 1593, a coalition of forces from the Croatian ban and the March and German troops (including divisions from the Slovene provinces under the command of Andrej of Auersperg-Turjak and Adam Ravbar) won a splendid victory over the Turks near Sisak. The victory was joyously celebrated in Croatia, in Slovene territories, and in Prague, then the capital of the Holy Roman Empire. This painful defeat provoked the Turks into a new war against the Hapsburgs lasting several years (1593-1606) during which they failed to conquer any new territory in Croatia and only a few areas in western Hungary. It became evident how important the Croatian March was from the military point of view. The March, at that time well furnished with a system of fortresses (Karlovac), prevented further Turkish raids into Slovene territory. It also became an important political and economic factor of development in the Inner Austrian, that is, largely Slovene provinces. These were obliged to collect the financial means necessary to maintain the March, whose supreme command was in Graz. The nobility of the Inner Austrian provinces were granted highly paid and prestigious officer posts in the March by the Hapsburgs who thus held in their hands an instrument for putting pressure on the nobility.

Initially, Archduke Ferdinand put pressure on the towns of Inner Austria. After a recatholicization plan had been prepared in advance, in 1598 he forbade Protestant services and education in all towns and boroughs. With military assistance, special Counter Reformation commissions headed by bishops (Ljubljana Bishop Tomaž Hren was responsible for Carniola) inspected the whole province, banished Protestant preachers, and burned Protestant books. Great damage was thus done to Slovene culture and the development of the Slovene language as the basis of the nation. The great majority of townspeople in Slovene territory renounced the Protestant faith, and only the wealthiest educated and religiously most zealous people emigrated to German Protestant countries. The

Slovene regions within the framework of the Holy Roman Empire at the beginning of the Thirty Years' War.

Archduke's plans to recatholicize the nobility were only interrupted for a short time by the new second Hapsburg-Venetian war, for which the Archduke needed the nobility's help. The war was triggered by the intense economic competition between Venice and Hapsburg Trieste. The war (1615-1617) only reached the marginal Slovene regions of Gorizia and Istria. It mainly took the form of devastating raids by the mercenary troops of one or the other side into enemy territory. The military successes alternated between the sides, and the peace treaty negotiated in Madrid in 1617 restored the original status quo. Though the Venetians withdrew from occupied territory, Venice had assured itself complete domination of the Adriatic for another hundred years.

After the death of his uncle Matthias in 1619, Inner Austria's Archduke Ferdinand inherited Upper and Lower Austria as well and was elected Emperor of the Holy Roman Empire. Using military force he fought resolutely with the Protestant Bohemian nobility that resisted acknowledging Ferdinand as King of Bohemia and with it recatholicization as well. The following year the Emperor defeated the Bohemians at the battle of White Mountain near Prague. Numerous Bohemian nobles and gentry were put to death or punished, their property was confiscated, and many emigrated to other European countries. Hapsburg absolutism and recatholiciza-tion were introduced In Bohemia, and the country was transformed into a Hapsburg crown land like other Austrian provinces.

Thus strengthened, Ferdinand undertook the recatholicization of the nobility in his Austrian provinces that included the Slovene territories and supported the recatholicization of Germany. The latter brought about the Thirty Years' War, and while in Germany (the Holy Roman Empire) the Emperor's power was diminished to the level of mere formality, he succeeded completely in his dynastic crown lands. Noblemen who refused to return to Catholicism after 1628 had to leave Styria, Carniola, and Carinthia, and within two years 750 members of noble families of higher or lower rank and property had left. The ruler granted or sold the confiscated property to noblemen coming from Catholic countries and to townspeople who had distinguished themselves in administrative service or in material acquisitions.

From the social viewpoint, this period of princely absolutism meant the greatest deterioration in the situation of the rural subjects. The absolutist prince excluded the nobility from political decisions in state affairs, but balanced this by giving them more power over the serfs which they used to impose increased tax burdens, especially the most hated socage. This situation remained unchanged until the middle of the 18th century when Enlightened Absolutism began to interfere decisively in the relationship between feudal lord and serf.

In the Austrian provinces the Counter Reformation was victorious, and a 150-year period of Catholic restoration and the rule of political absolutism began. From the political, national, and cultural viewpoint, this period meant a certain stagnation or even regression for the Slovenes compared to the era of the Reformation.

The Protestants had foreseen an elementary school in every parish but did not have enough time to realize this vision. Protestantism built its concept on man, on the individual, and on the nation of the new religion and was therefore more receptive toward national and cultural development than the Catholic revival movement that based its actions on the Church community and Catholic universalism. The Catholic revival movement conceived the elementary school as an institution only for those who would be further educated later. Bishop Hren of Ljubljana, a fervent supporter of the Catholic revival, received Vatican permission for the Jesuit Janez Čandek to adapt parts of Dalmatin's translation of the *Bible* for the needs of the liturgy and to publish them in the book *Gospels and Readings* in 1613. Two years later, Čandek also published *A Small Catechism* by Peter Kanizij, but after that no book was printed in the Slovene language for sixty years.

The general cultural and scientific development in Slovene territories fared much better, and in the 17th century several important historical and natural science works appeared in German and Latin. The most significant and most famous was the extensive natural science, ethnographic, topographic, and historical work *Glory of the Duchy of Carniola* (Die Ehre des Hertzogthums Crain) by the nobleman Janez Vajkard Valvasor that was published in Nürnberg in 1689; it was similar to similar patriotic works of its type in other Austrian lands. Because of his studies of the intermittent Cerknica Lake, Valvasor was admitted to the English Royal Academy of Science. Shortly before Valvasor, the Jesuit Martin Baučer had written about the history of the Friuli and Gorizia regions. Valvasor's contemporary Janez Schönleben wrote about the older history of Ljubljana (Emona). In the first half of the 18th century, the Carinthian Slovene historian Marko Hanžič dealt with the history of Carinthia in the framework of the history of Salzburg.

In 1701, a group of Ljubljana intelligentsia (twelve lawyers, six theologians, and five medical men) following the Italian example founded the *Academia Operosorum Labacensium* which subsequently functioned for a quarter of a century, its work spanning all branches of knowledge it represented.

In the decades of the 18th century, the Hapsburg Monarchy, for which the name "Austrian Monarchy" was introduced in official documents in 1711, was involved in two exhausting wars: the War of the Spanish (Hapsburg) Succession (1701-1713) and the war with rebellious Hungarian States (1700-1711). In the first war, the peace treaty gave Austria the Spanish possessions in Italy, in particular the Duchy of Milan that was very important for the future of Austria as it became a decisive power in Italian politics for 150 years. The war with the Hungarian rebels led by Prince Ferenc Rákóczi ended in 1711 with a peace that gave the Hungarian States greater political autonomy and religious freedom but once more confirmed the Hapsburgs as their rulers. Under Emperor Karl VI, Austria exploited its stronger position in Italy to advantage by proclaiming free navigation in the Adriatic in 1717, which Venice was obliged to accept. Two years later, Trieste and Rijeka were proclaimed free ports and the Eastern Company was founded in Vienna. All this affected the position of Slovene territories in the Austrian Monarchy.

An improved road link between Vienna and Trieste via Graz, Maribor, Celje, Trojane, and Ljubljana was begun. A second traffic route across Slovene territory was also built along the Sava River by regulating its riverbed and constructing a riverside path for towing barges from Ljubljana to Zagreb. The mercantile state policy and the need to supply the Croatian March still under Austrian command enabled the development of manufacturing in Slovenia: forges at Jesenice and in Bohinj, a state textile mill in Ljubljana, many companies in Trieste, etc. Rich merchants and businessmen from northern Italy and the Austrian and Bohemian provinces settled in Slovene territories and soon mixed with the provincial town population to become important supporters of development (e.g., the Ruard, Codelli, Zois, and Schellenburg families).

In the first half of the 18th century there was exceptionally intense construction activity in Slovene territories, largely in the baroque style. The majority of towns such as Ljubljana, Maribor, and Klagenfurt thus acquired their baroque appearance. In this period many churches and aristocratic manor houses were built or renovated. Ljubljana alone got three beautiful baroque churches: the Cathedral, the Church of the Cross, and the church of the Ursuline Order joined the church of the Augustine Monastery built at the end of the 17th century. The builders were several eminent Italian architects such as Andrea Pozzo (the

Ljubljana Cathedral) from whom many Slovene masters such as Gregor Maček (the Ljubljana Town Hall and numerous baroque churches throughout the Slovene countryside) received their education. Baroque painting (frescoes as well as oil paintings) developed highly in Slovenia, and several Slovene painters such as Fran Jelovšek and Fortunat Bergant achieved enviable artistic heights.

8. The Enlightenment and the National Revival

During the first known census in the Hapsburg Monarchy in the middle of the 18th century, the Slovene population numbered less than one million. Between 1747 and 1749 at the end of the first decade of her reign, Maria Theresa began to establish a new official state administration in her Austrian crown lands with a sort of provincial government and a lower administrative hierarchy of departments. She abolished customs barriers between provinces and thus united the economy into a state unit. Great attention was devoted to improving transportation routes, especially those that linked Vienna across Slovene territory to Trieste. As a result, the populations of Slovene regions from Šentilj to Trieste and from Carinthia to Croatia were better connected and awareness grew of the extent and unity of Slovene ethnic territory. Throughout the Monarchy and in its Slovene regions as well, the development of manufacturing intensified. In each region farm cooperatives were concerned with the development of modern farming and introduced new plants, in particular potatoes, corn, and clover. Keeping livestock in stables made it possible to manure the fields and abandon three-year crop rotation. Epoch-making changes took place in agriculture that made larger crops possible and provided the basis to support an increasing population. Through state legislation, Enlightened Absolutism attempted to regulate and improve the social position of its rural subjects by encouraging the transition of remaining subject farms to hereditary holdings.

From the beginning of the 1770's, the state considered education, and in 1774 with an imperial decree actually introduced a three-year elementary school to teach its population the reading, writing, and arithmetic necessary for prudent farming, factory work, and military service. In spite of its centralistic character and its desire to unify the state educationally and culturally through the German language, there was sufficient pragmatism in the political circles of Maria Theresa that the three-year elementary schools were allowed to function in the language the population understood, that is, in Slovene in Slovene regions. Thus the Slovene elementary school came into being, the plan for which had already been submitted to Maria Theresa in 1772 by the Slovene teacher Blaž Kumardej. The elementary school, which only slowly made its influence felt, became one of the most important foundations of the Slovene national revival.

A second important social act of the Enlightenment provided a further basis for the growth and development of the Slovene national revival. In 1782, Emperor Joseph II passed a decree giving the serfs their personal freedom and opened the door for the gradual formation of the Slovene middle class that would become the main pillar of the modern Slovene nation. Along with all these objective social, economic, and political conditions, the subjective will and determination of a handful of Slovene intellectuals was extremely important for the beginning of a cultural campaign to raise the Slovene language to the same level as German and Italian. The Slovenes would thus be able to receive the achievements of European culture in their own language and to contribute in their own language to this culture as well. One result of such thinking was the grammar book published by the Carniolan grammarian and priest Marko Pohlin in 1768. In 1784, Ljubljana's Bishop Herberstein, who was well known in Europe as the ideologist behind Joseph II's religious reforms, inspired a new Slovene translation of the *Bible* that his secretary Jurij Japelj published over the following twenty years. In his work Japelj could lean on Dalmatin's translation, but he modernized the language and extended it with the Gorenjska dialect.

In addition to the clerical revivalist circle, a secular circle was gathering around the wealthy Baron Žiga Zois who encouraged national revival and cultural work. Members of this circle included the poet and priest Valentin Vodnik; Anton Tomaž Linhart, an official of the Ljubljana departmental office, lawyer, historian, and dramatist; Baltazar Hacquet, a doctor and botanist of French origin; and several others.

Between 1788 and 1791, Anton Tomaž Linhart, the most important member of this circle, published the first scientific history of Slovenes in two parts, written from the viewpoint of Slovene national integrity, in which he identified the extent and unity of the Slovene nation. Introducing his work in the newspaper *Laibacher Zeitung* in 1786, he explained "What are we Carniolans?" as follows: "The nation living in the southern part of the Austrian department between the Drau River and the Adriatic Sea belongs to the great characteristic limb of the Slav people who according to their language and origin are one and the same branch of people and are only by accident although historically not quite exactly divided into Carniolans and Vinds (Slovenes)". Linhart did not use the term "Vinds" (Slovenes) but rather "Kranjci" (Carniolans) and "Karantanci" which he derived from Karantanija, the first Slovene state, to which he devoted considerable space in his book. In his attempt at history he only covered from the oldest periods of life on Slovene territory up to the fall of independent Karantanija or the death of Charlemagne. Through its progressive contents and its linking of the Slovenes as a whole, Linhart's work was the greatest cultural act of the Slovene national awakening in the 18th century. The emphasis in his work was placed on the history of civilization and the life of people and not on political and military events or descriptions of rulers. Simply by referring to the importance of the development of the people, Linhart refuted the assertion that the Slovenes had no history. As the first Slovene historian, he rejected the presentation of Slovene history according to provinces and considered the division of the Slovenes into provinces as the result of historical development. The immediate fruit of this work was the recognition of the ethnic identity of the whole Slovene nation. Even before Linhart's death in 1795, this recognition had been accepted by Kumardej and Japelj, and Jernej Kopitar strengthened it among international linguistic circles with the publication of his remarkable German-language *Grammar of the Slovene Language in Carniola, Carinthia, and Styria* in 1808. From then on, the term "Slovenci" (Slovenes) was established, for which Vodnik and Janez Nepomuk Primic also deserve credit along with Kopitar.

Linhart's contribution to the development of Slovene literature is also very important. He wrote the first two Slovene plays, *Županova Micka* (The Burgomaster's Micka) in 1789 and *Ta veseli dan* or *Matiček se ženi*" (That Happy Day or The Marriage of Matiček) in 1790. Because of its progressive anti-feudal content, the latter was banned until the revolutionary year of 1848. Besides Linhart, the man who contributed most to the development of Slovene literature and national awareness was Valentin Vodnik, who wrote poetry and in 1797 established *Lublanske novice* (The Ljubljana News), the first Slovene newspaper. With the founding of *Lublanske novice* two years after Linhart's death, the first phase of the Slovene national revival came to an end; however, it was followed by two more: the period of the Illyrian Provinces and the period before the March Revolution.

In addition to national awakening thought and action, much happened generally in the second half of the 18th century in the field of arts and sciences as many from Slovene territories made their names in other provinces of the Austrian Monarchy. Let us mention only Franc Karpet from Ljubljana, a philosophy professor at the universities of Olomouc, Brno, and Vienna where he was a well-known supporter of the Enlightenment and a disciple of Kant. In Carniola itself, two eminent physicians and natural scientists were active: J.K. Scopoli and the Frenchman Baltazar Hacquet. Hacquet was first a surgeon at the Idrija mercury mine and later a professor of anatomy, surgery, and midwifery at the medical school in Ljubljana. He became famous for studying the geology and flora of the whole Slovene territory. In 1787 he left Ljubljana to become professor of natural sciences at the University in L'vov in Ukraine. The brothers Žiga and Karl Zois were well-known across Europe, the first as a mineralogist and the latter as a botanist. Of Slovene origin as well was the Austrian artillery officer and mathematician Jurij Vega who in 1792 wrote a handbook of logarithmic tables that was regularly reprinted throughout the Monarchy in the following century. Commissioned by the provincial government of Carniola, the Jesuit G. Grubar built a major canal to divert the waters of the Ljubljanica River around the town behind the castle, making possible the draining of the Ljubljana Barje moor and preventing the river from flooding the town. In the southeastern part of Ljubljana he erected a beautiful baroque palace with a wonderful rococo chapel, painted by the famous artist Kremser-Schmidt.

9. The Illyrian Provinces and the Period before the March Revolution of 1848

On the threshold of the 19th century, Slovene regions too felt the effects of the Napoleonic Wars. Napoleon entered Slovene territory the first time in 1797, crossing it in pursuit of the Austrian army retreating from Italy to Leoben. On this occasion he issued an appeal to the Slovenes (whom he called Carniolans) for neutrality in the struggle of the French Republic with the English and the Vienna government, promising to respect their religion, customs, and property.

The second time, the French occupied almost all of Slovene territory after their victory over Austria and Russia in the battle near Slavkovo in 1805. This time they imposed sizable reparations on Slovene provinces, and with the peace treaty signed in Bratislava in December 1805 they secured from Austria all the Venetian provinces including Istria which Austria had acquired less than a decade earlier with the peace treaty in Campoformido.

After his third victory over Austria near Wagram in 1809, Napoleon cut off Austria from the Adriatic by creating the Illyrian Provinces from several Slovene and Croatian regions, linking them across Italy with the French Empire. The Slovene regions of western Carinthia, Carniola, Gorizia, Trieste, and Istria (which was populated by Slovenes, Croatians, and Italians) belonged to the Illyrian Provinces along with Croatia south of the Sava River and Dalmatia. For the Provinces the French invented an antique name by analogy with other marginal territories connected with France. Ljubljana became their capital. Over two thirds of Slovene territory thus came under French authority for four years. The French did not introduce the French Constitution in the Illyrian Provinces, but instead merely replaced the feudal administration with French administration at the lowest levels of the hierarchy and applied the *Code Napoléon*. Thus feudal rule was struck a heavy blow and all its public legal rights were annulled. However, the French were unable to carry out the final step they had planned, the total abolition of feudal rule and serfdom, and the social position of the Slovene rural population did not improve. For this reason and because of the high reparations demanded, the peasants were left with bad memories of French authority. The Slovene provinces also suffered economically due to the continental blockade in the period of French rule. Because the border with Austria was closed, the production of iron declined and trade via Rijeka and Trieste was reduced by 90%.

With regard to national and cultural development, the Illyrian Provinces appear in a more positive light. In the period of their existence, the Slovene language gained importance in public use. According to the plan for the organization of schools of May 30, 1810, authored by Valentin Vodnik, the principle was established that young Illyrians (Slovenes) be allowed education in their mother tongue while at the same time also learning French and Italian. The younger circle of Slovene national revivalists was enthusiastic about the plan, and Vodnik even wrote the ode "Illyria Revived" in honour of Napoleon. During the years of the French rule, Vodnik wrote nearly all the textbooks for Slovene primary schools, which was of great importance for later times as well. The French also introduced Slovene in place of German in Ljubljana's upper elementary schools and tried to do the same in lower secondary school classes. In the upper secondary classes they attempted to introduce French and Italian, but in spite of this restriction the position of Slovene schools under the French was only improved upon after 1848.

After Napoleon's defeat near Leipzig in October 1813, the French abandoned the Illyrian Provinces and the Austrian authorities returned and restored the old feudal and political systems. Metternich's Absolutism opposed all nationalist political movements among the nations in the Austrian Monarchy. Thus, in the period before the March Revolution the Slovenes were unable to further their national political movement and program. However, they developed their language and cultural activity intensively. This was encouraged as much by conservative Slovenes (Kopitar, Slomšek, Koseski, Bleiweis) as by liberal Slovenes (Prešeren, Smole).

The conservative Styrian (Štajerska) priest Anton Martin Slomšek was a man of simple peasant origins, and all his life and even as a bishop he remained true to his people and their needs, understanding them in his own way from the Christian Catholic religious, anthropological, and moral point of view. He encouraged them to be faithful to the Slovene language, saying that before God all nations and all languages were equal and that there was no difference between a German and a Slovene. He also maintained that it was our duty not only to preserve the language we received from our parents but also to make it even more beautiful and to pass it on to our children: "Whoever forgets his Slovene mother tongue buries his talent wickedly; one day God will demand his answer and all those who scorn their honest language will be thrust into outer darkness!"

Slomšek wrote a number of books for Slovene schoolchildren as well as simple heartfelt poems that became popular. His later Church activities were of great importance in strengthening the Slovene identity in Styria, but as he was a conservative and a legitimist, it would be too much to expect him to have supported the radical Slovene national and political program.

In Carniola we can parallel Slomšek with Janez Bleiweis, a veterinary surgeon and secretary of the Agricultural Society. He was above all a practical specialist who did not show any political ambitions and the authorities trusted him. In 1843, Bleiweis received permission to publish a Slovene newspaper, *Kmetijske in rokodelske novice* (Farming and Handicraft News), the first since 1797. Editing *Kmetijske in rokodelske novice*, Bleiweis very quickly established his position among the Slovenes and to some extent became their central figure. From Slovene cultural figures he invited conservatives to work for his newspaper, in particular Ivan Vesel-Koseski, who was not a great artistic talent but wrote patriotic poems. With his 1844 poem "Slovenia to Emperor

Ferdinand on his Name Day," Vesel-Koseski established himself forever in the memory of Slovenes as he was the first to clearly and in its full extent call their country "Slovenia." In the poem, which glorified the illustrious history of the country, he also expressed the message of Slovene conservatism: steadfast loyalty to the Emperor at all cost.

Even more important for national development was the liberal circle that gathered around the poet Franc Prešeren and resolved some of the basic dilemmas of Slovene national development of the time. In the middle of the 1830's, Prešeren and his colleagues succeeded in defending the unity of the Slovene language and thus the nation's foundation against attempts to establish various regional dialects as the literary standard, a separate one for Styria and a separate one for Carniola. Then followed the settling of accounts with those disheartened Slovenes who proposed mixing the Slovene language with Croatian, thus drowning the Slovene nation in the Croatian. This concept called "Illyrism" maintained that all Southern Slav nations were really one single nation. It was politically conceived at the beginning of the 1830's in Croatia and was intended to serve the interests of the Croatian national and political movement. The Illyrian ideal resurfaced among the Slovenes in various forms from time to time for another one hundred years.

Prešeren resolved yet another essential issue in the development of the Slovene nation. Through his excellent poetic creations (comparable to those of his European contemporaries), he raised Slovene culture and the Slovene language to a level that made possible the expression of the highest works of artistic and scientific creation, a precondition for the integration of the middle classes in the Slovene linguistic cultural circle. Without the middle class Slovenes would have been left without the elite that was the pillar of the Slovene nationalist movement in the later 19th century.

Prešeren and the members of his circle were politically conscious and longed for a more independent Slovene national life, a wish Prešeren expressed in his poem "Zdravljica" (A Toast):

> Now, as it once had striven,
> May our dear realm in freedom grow.
> May fall the last
> Chains of the past
> Which bind us still and hold us fast!

He also expressed the liberal spirit of brother-hood among nations:

> God's blessing on all nations,
> Who long and work for that bright day,
> When o'er earth's habitations
> No war, no strife shall hold its sway;
> Who long to see
> That all men free
> No more shall foes, but neighbours be.

(translation by Janko Lavrin, *A Selection of Poems by France Prešeren*, Basil Blackwell, *Oxford 1954*).

One hundred and fifty years later, this inspiring poem became the national anthem of the independent Slovene state.

However, in the Hapsburg Monarchy of the time, inspiring thoughts could not replace a truly concrete Slovene national and political program, and this was only born in the March Revolution of 1848. In spite of the lack of activity at the political level in the period before the March Revolution, Slovene regions displayed the first clearly visible evidence of modernization. The number of people living in towns was growing, and several modern factories had been built, primarily the spinning and textile mills in Prebold, Ljubljana, and Ajdovščina and the large sugar refinery in Ljubljana. These were joined by modern factories in Trieste and Koper and by modern financial and commercial companies. The most important harbinger of the new industrial era was the construction of the Southern Railway from Vienna to Trieste, which by 1846 had already reached as far as Celje.

III. ENDEAVOURS FOR A UNITED SLOVENIA WITHIN THE HAPSBURG MONARCHY

10. The March Revolution of 1848 and the Birth of the Program of the United Slovenia

The Slovenes learned very quickly about the March Revolution that had swept away Metternich's absolutist regime in Vienna, since the railway already ran as far as the middle of Slovene territory. The people in Slovene regions reacted the same way as people elsewhere in the Monarchy. Townspeople welcomed the political change in the capital and the promise of a constitution and political rights and established civic or so-called "national" guards to maintain order and security. In the Slovene countryside, the peasants interpreted the change in the regime as the end of feudal rule. In some places they broke into manor houses, burned land registers (Ig near Ljubljana), and attacked and destroyed the tollhouses outside the towns that had hindered their trade. It can be said that the bourgeois Revolution of 1848 triggered the final Slovene peasant uprising against the feudal system, which together with similar movements all over the Monarchy brought about the final abolition of the feudal system with the Emperor's *Manifesto* in September 1848.

For Slovene national development it was of utmost significance that various groups of Slovenes as well as several individuals drafted and published Slovene national and political programs. The first two, the program of the

Slovene intellectuals in Vienna and the program of Matija Majer-Ziljski, the curate of the cathedral in Klagenfurt, were published in 1848. In slightly different words the two programs demanded essentially the same thing, that is, the unification of all Slovene regions into one province, a "United Slovenia" in which Slovene would be the official language and the language used in schools. Still within the framework of the Austrian Monarchy, this Slovene province would enjoy a certain degree of national autonomy through its own provincial assembly. This program, published in similar texts by other Slovene groups in Graz, Ljubljana, and Trieste, was commonly called the "United Slovenia Program" and became the political program of the Slovenes for the following one hundred years.

The program was based on the democratic foundation of human and national equality, on the basis of natural though not historical law, but in the Austria of that time such principles were not victorious. Austria's German-speaking bourgeoisie and its conservative elite who were prepared to compromise with the Hungarian and Italian provinces and Polish Galicia rejected any autonomy for the Czechs and the Slovenes. These were considered normal constituent parts of German Austria and in the opinion of the liberal bourgeoisie they should have been included in the great German state which the committee in Frankfurt pleaded for. In a letter by their eminent leader František Palacki, the Czechs decisively refused to be included in the "Frankfurt" Germany and immediately afterwards the Slovenes did the same. In the revolutionary year of 1848, the Slovenes did not have any effective instruments of power to realize their political program; they did not have their own military regiments because of which Austria would have been prepared for concessions as was the case with Croatia; and they did not have any political representation to defend the Slovene national interest. They developed major political propaganda against the May elections to the Frankfurt Parliament, the result of which was that in some constituencies elections were not even held and in others representatives were elected by only a handful of votes. In one item of his famous program "What do we Slovenes demand?" Matija Majer-Ziljski wrote: "We do not want to be in the German Union (*Deutscher Bund*), no matter what it costs. We are and want to be faithful to our most illustrious Emperor and to our constitutional government, we want to be and stay in friendly relations with all nations of our Empire, including the Germans, but with Germany and its foreign rulers we have therefore nothing to do. Any links with those Germans would obviously harm us."

Dr. Josip Kranjc, senior law lecturer at the University of Graz and one of the wisest political heads among the Slovenes in 1848, similarly wrote against Frankfurt. In his polemics with the Germans who had doubts about the possibility of Slovene national development, he expressed some thoughts which best reflect the constant existential dilemma of the Slovenes. He wrote that the Slovenes would not commit suicide for fear of death. He maintained it was impossible to deny any nation the right to protect its basic rights, no matter how annoying that might be for some. He radically refused a Greater Germany: "If a German brother in Austria wants to go where his home is but where a Slovene is a foreigner, we will not stop him. Let him move from us and establish a border decided on an ethnic basis." From this the geographer Peter Kozler was motivated to begin preparing an exact statistical geographical study of the Slovene ethnic border. His exceptionally precise field-work together with a map was published only in 1853.

In May, at the initiative of the Slovenes in Vienna, Slovene political societies began to collect signatures for a United Slovenia in order to forward them to the Emperor. The campaign had great success, especially in Styria, and in the autumn of 1848 the petition was sent to the National Assembly in Kromeriž (Kremsier). Through the autumn national tensions between Germans and Slovenes increased. The German point of view was formulated the most clearly by the Vincenz Rizzi, a German liberal from Carinthia: "We understand that in spite of all political equality and brotherly communication with the Germans, an educated Slovene will never really feel at ease in a German Union. We understand because we have experienced ourselves what tribal love is, because our heart teaches us to come to know and respect the Slovene heart. But to all cravings for separation we too have only one word as an answer, a sad, inexorable one – political necessity. The possession of Trieste and passage to it is a vital question for Germany – this is its only southern port." This attitude of the German population in the Hapsburg Monarchy towards the position of the Slovenes and Slovene regions remained constant until the dissolution of the Monarchy at the end of World War I, and to a large extent it determined the politics of the Slovene nation and its political factors.

In the Kromeriž Parliament, Ludwig Löhner, a deputy of the German left wing, suggested the reorganization of Austria into a federation of national units whose borders would be defined according to ethnic borders. One of the units would have been Slovene Austria, but this suggestion remained only an episode of the revolutionary year of 1848.

In 1848 the Slovenes were unable to realize their well considered and perspective program, and it remained only a prospect for the future, for new social and political circumstances. However, in 1848 the Slovenes achieved recognition of their ethnic individuality, name, and integrity, and when by decree farmers were no longer bound to their feudal lords and the nobility's monopoly in political life was abolished, the possibility was born for the Slovene nation to enter political life. The year 1848 was therefore one of the most important turning points in Slovene history.

The decade following the March Revolution is known as the decade of Bach Absolutism. In this period without constitutional and democratic rights the Slovenes could not be politically active. But under the political surface, times were not so bad. The land redemption was actually carried out and indemnity money fixed which the farmers had to pay on state holidays in the following two decades. The country was administratively divided into municipalities (which were the basic cells in the development of political democracy in the future) and districts. Industry continued to develop, and the Southern Railway reached Trieste in 1857.

The introduction of a constitution and political democracy in Austria was to the advantage of the Slovenes, and general political and national awareness grew. This was clearly reflected during the elections to the provincial assemblies in 1867. A sort of Slovene national party was victorious in the elections to the Carniolan provincial assembly, while in the provincial assemblies of Styria, Carinthia, Gorizia, and Trieste where it was represented it increased the number of its representatives; their number stayed basically the same to the end of the Monarchy. Such great success inclined the liberal Dr. Valentin Zarnik, one of the Slovene political leaders, to write: "Only now can we breathe freely, only now can we say that the Slovene nation really exists, that it lives, that it has matured politically, and that we are no longer just an ethnic notion.

In 1868, under the influence of the Czechs, the leaders of the Slovene national movement decided to organize mass rallies under the open sky; originally they were called "meetings" after the English, but the Czech term "*tabori*" soon became popular. Slovene politicians saw these mass rallies as an instrument of political pressure on the ruling circles in the Monarchy so that in the democratic spirit they would satisfy the Slovenes and allow them the unification of Slovene regions in an autonomous United Slovenia within the Monarchy. A second demand that appeared at nearly all the rallies was the

Nationalities in the western part of the Hapsburg Monarchy

demand that all subjects in Slovene primary and secondary schools be taught in the Slovene language, and very often they also demanded the foundation of a special law faculty or even a university in Slovene territory. They also wanted Slovene to become the administrative language for the highest provincial offices in Slovene territory and even demanded that Slovene soldiers be commanded in the Slovene language. At every mass rally they also had specific local economic and cultural demands. The first *tabor* was held in Ljutomer on August 9, 1868, and some 10,000 people attended. *Tabors* were organized for the next three years. All together there were thirty-four in all the Slovene regions. The largest was at Vižmarje near Ljubljana on May 17, 1869, when between 25,000 and 30,000 people gathered. Every level of Slovene society participated in the *tabors* especially the farmers and bourgeoisie. Ideological and political differences did not hinder them, and the *tabors* were therefore a sort of pan-national plebiscite for a United Slovenia in which the whole nation appeared united, a union that appeared later only twice. Immediately following the *tabors*, political differentiation appeared.

In the middle of the 1860's, history struck the Slovenes a hard blow. After losing the war with Prussia, in 1866 Austria had to cede Slovene Venetia to Prussia's ally Italy. The Venetia Slovenes were thus cut off from their mother country and became an unprotected minority in the Italian state. In every respect, this 2% of the Slovenes developed under much more unfavourable conditions than the Slovenes in Austria, and their national movement was weak.

11. Economic, Social, and Cultural Development in Slovenia in the Last Third of the 19th Century

The last third of the 19th century was a period of rapid and many-sided development in Slovenia. On one hand, it was a period of severe economic crisis in agriculture because of the added burden arising from the farmers' obligations to their previous feudal lords, indemnity money owed for children leaving the farms, and a surplus rural population that could not find employment in the too slowly developing industries. It was therefore a period of major emigration of the surplus population to other countries in Europe and to North America. For this reason, the Slovene nation developed demographically in this period more slowly than other European nations. On the other hand, at the beginning of this period two major industrial enterprises were established that held an important place in the Slovene economy for the next hundred years: the Carniola Industrial Association (*Kranjska industrijska družba*) with ironworks in Jesenice and the Trbovlje Colliery Association (Trboveljska premogokopna družba). Owing to the lack of domestic capital, by the end of the century German and French capital were firmly anchored in both enterprises. Another very important industrial plant with the biggest number of qualified workers was the Maribor Railway Works (Mariborske železniške delavnice), the largest on the Southern Railway line between Graz and Trieste. Of course, we must also mention the exceptionally rapid industrial development of Trieste, which was situated in Slovene ethnic territory although two thirds of its residents were Italians who largely comprised the upper ruling classes.

In this period the Slovene nation achieved such rapid and obvious cultural and educational progress that it convinced the nationalist German sociologist Gumplowicz (a professor at the University of Graz) that with such cultural development the Slovene nation had proved its capacity for survival and its right to live in the Hapsburg Monarchy.

At the end of the century there was a network of elementary schools across Slovene territory, and among the nations of the Monarchy the level of literacy among Slovenes followed the literacy levels of the Germans and the Czechs. In secondary schools and teacher training colleges, Slovene was only slowly asserting itself, especially in the lower classes. But the Slovenes had to fight hard for every achievement, even directly with the government in Vienna. In 1895 the issue of introducing parallel Slovene classes in the secondary school in Celje became such a major political problem that it even caused the fall of Prime Minister Windischgrätz.

The cultural conception that elite grammar schools clearly formed the national awareness of a national elite guided the ruling German circles and until the end of the Monarchy they did not allow the establishment of even one completely Slovene state secondary school. In 1904 the first private parochial Slovene secondary school was established in Ljubljana.

In the last third of the 19th century, the Slovenes showed great cultural and artistic creativity that followed Central and Western European cultural currents. At the end of the century, Slovene literature that demonstrated great achievements in Realism followed modern European models, and its two greatest representatives – Cankar, the greatest Slovene writer, and Župančič – had already published their first books. Slovene realist painting was on the European level as well, and one of its representatives, Anton Ažbe, had a very well known school of painting in Munich open to new streams of art from which several famous painters of European Impressionism and Symbolism arose. Especially in Impressionist painting a number of Slovenes created great works of art at the end of the 19th century so that the Slovene national ideology proclaimed that Impressionism was the style corresponding to the Slovene spirit.

At the end of the 19th century, the new Christian Social movement with its capable organizer of social and economic life on principles of solidarity in the form of cooperative self-help, Janez Evangelist Krek, succeeded considerably in improving the lot of the farmers so that they no longer sold their farms and emigration was greatly reduced. The Christian Social movement also organized social self-help and an educational organization for workers as well, thus competing with the slightly older socialist Marxist Workers movement.

At the end of the century, the Slovene nation was politically organized in three political parties – the Catholic National Party, the Liberal Party, and the Social Democratic Party – which differed in their social bases and very strongly in their ideas and political orientation. The relationship among them was that of an irreconcilable political battle that intensified their ideological differences on nearly all issues of Slovene national development.

At the end of the 19th century, deliberate and severe imperialist pressure doubled on Slovene territory. From the north attempts were made to establish a German "bridge" to Trieste, while from the west the Irredentist movement in Italy laid claim to parts of Slovene territory (Gorizia, Trieste, Istria). This pressure began to cut away at the borders of Slovene ethnic territory.

Although the Slovene nation had neither its administrative territorial unity nor national or political autonomy, it was still possible at the end of the 19th century to speak of the Slovenes as a completely formed nation in the modern sense of Renan's definition of a nation as an everyday plebiscite. This definition was reflected in the national and political awareness of all classes and in their demand for a politically autonomous United Slovenia and their opposition to German rule.

12. Slovene Political Endeavours from the End of the 19th Century to World War I

At the end of the 19th century, the Slovene political and cultural elite were permeated by the fear of the pressure of Germanization. They believed that they could resist this pressure only with a nationally and politically autonomous United Slovenia that would include all the provinces settled by a majority of Slovenes distinguished from the Germans and Italians by the clearly visible ethnic borders that had been formed from the period of the planned denationalization of Slovene territory to the beginning of imperialism. In 1890 in this Slovene ethnic territory, which corresponded closely to the 1848 vision of the United Slovenia, lived 90% of the Slovene population from a total nearly one and a half million Slovenes. However, this figure is not completely reliable since in the census the language of intercourse was considered and not the mother tongue. Thus many townspeople in Carinthia and Styria as well as in Trieste who were Slovenes and had come from the Slovene countryside only a few years before cited the German that they used in public because of social prestige and political pressure as their language of intercourse.

Until 1897, the Catholic National Party, the leading Slovene political power, built its strategy of establishing an autonomous United Slovenia with the help of the ideologically related German Christian Social Party. But the failure of Bedeni's language reforms that the German Christian Socialists opposed opened the eyes of the Catholic National Party. It parted from its old political allies and began to look for a new way to solve the Slovene national question, a United Slovenia within the Hapsburg Monarchy. It decided on political cooperation and links with Croatia's Party of Justice (Stranka prava) that was striving to establish a large Croatian state within the framework of the Hapsburg Monarchy. Slovene Catholic politicians calculated that with the help of the Croats and their better national and political status and by adopting the Croatian political program they could solve the Slovene national question. They thought they might al least restrain German and Italian nationalist and imperialist pressure on the Slovenes. Emphasizing this point, Slovene Catholic politicians and later the Liberals as well bowed to the political concept of uniting the Slovenes with a Croatian state that would become a third unit of the Hapsburg Monarchy – *Trialism*. This decision had fateful and long-term consequences for Slovene national development. Although some political circles in Vienna including the Christian Social Party and Crown Prince Ferdinand favoured trialism since it would include only the Croats and thus weaken the Hungarians, but under no circumstances would the Slovenes be included because they were considered part of the narrower Austrian German-speaking territorial sphere. In spite of the prevailing view in Vienna, the Slovenes clung to this political concept because they had nothing better or more realistic. Emphasizing national brotherhood and solidarity with the Croats (Slovene Liberals also included the Orthodox Serbs in this solidarity) was probably the only possible Slovene political strategy in the given situation. Several political and cultural circles in all political camps among the Slovenes believed in the national and cultural fusion of all Southern Slav nations before World War I. These utopian cultural ideas were never accepted by the mass of the Slovene people, and they were also rejected by Ivan Cankar, one of the greatest Slovene writers, who was also very politically and socially astute. In his 1913 essay "Slovenes and the Southern Slavs" he pointed out the great differences in culture and civilization between the Slovenes and other Southern Slav nations that had been created by more than a thousand years of development with the result that the Slovenes had developed into a Western European nation even though their language was related to the languages of other Southern Slav nations. Cankar also stated that there was no common Southern Slav culture and that it was impossible to form a new Yugoslav nation. He suggested only a joint political project, a federal republic of Southern Slavs. In the following years, Cankar's lucid cultural analysis was forgotten by some Slovene politicians.

13. World War I – the Secession of the Slovenes from Austria

During World War I, the Slovenes experienced growing political pressure not only from internal enemies in the Monarchy but also from external enemies. Italian imperialist pressure from outside threatened the existence of the Slovenes, especially after the London Agreement between Italy and the Triple Entente in April of 1915. For entering the war on the side of the Entente, Italy was promised a great deal of Hapsburg territory including South Tyrol, Trentino, and Slovene Primorska (Gorizia and Trieste) and spreading even farther eastwards into parts of Carniola, Istria, and Dalmatia. Slovene appeals to Russia for its political intervention against the Entente and for the protection of the integrity of the Slovene territory had no effect. For this reason, Slovenes on the

Russian front surrendered to captivity while on the Soča (Isonzo) front they fought bravely in the Austrian army because they felt they were defending their own land, the whole of Slovenia, against the intention of Italy to occupy parts of Slovenia and dismember it.

In the spring of 1916, Slovene national and political prospects worsened when the German political parties in Austria demanded in their political platforms an immediate constitutional act that would transform half of the whole Austrian state into a German state. The death warrant would have been written for the Czech and Slovene nations.

The Slovenes could not even protest politically against such intentions: the political bodies in which they had seats such as the Provincial Assemblies and the Vienna Parliament were not in session because of the state of war, and political publications were sharply censored. In such a situation the Slovene political leadership headed by Janez Evangelist Krek and Anton Korošec again sought help from the Croatian Party of Justice. They knew they had to act at once to achieve some solution to the national situation while the war was still going on and the Slovene nation still had some political weight in the Monarchy as a reservoir of military forces. With the support of Croatian Party of Justice politicians, the Slovenes succeeded in uniting all the delegates from the Southern Slav regions in the Vienna Parliament (Slovenia, Istria, and Dalmatia) into the Yugoslav Deputies Club. At its first wartime session on May 30, 1917, it read its political demands as had other Austrian nations. The so-called "May Declaration" only more radically and clearly repeated the old Slovene and Croatian trialist demands. On the basis of the national principle and Croatian state rights, it demanded the immediate union of all territories in the Monarchy where Slovenes, Croats, and Serbs lived (Slovenia, Croatia, Dalmatia, Bosnia and Herzegovina, and Vojvodina) into one united and independent state body on democratic principles under the sceptre of the Hapsburg Dynasty. The demands of the May Declaration were nationally and politically revolutionary since they demanded the abolition of the Dual Monarchy, changes in the constitution, and the establishment of a third Yugoslav unit within the Monarchy. The Declaration was not supported by any important ruling elements in the Hapsburg Monarchy, nor by the Austrian and Hungarian governments, the Hungarian and German parties, or by the royal court itself.

In the autumn of 1917, the Slovene national leadership organized a pan-Slovene campaign in support of the May Declaration. By the spring of 1918, more than 250,000 signatures, mostly women's, had been collected. People all over Slovenia signed, even municipality councils, at the strong opposition of the Styrian Germans. The Yugoslav Deputies Club sent its memorandum also to the peace conference in Brest-Litovsk, with a demand that the rights of the Yugoslav nations to self-determination be considered. Since June 1917, the May Declaration had been supported in the Croatian parliament only by the minority Party of Justice while the majority Croatian-Serbian coalition, having other political plans, showed total indifference. The impossibility of reaching an agreement with the ruling elite in Vienna only incited greater radicalism and opposition to Austria in Slovene national politics.

In the spring of 1918, the Slovene leadership decided on total separation from the Hapsburg Monarchy. The Slovenes were most worried that Austrian policies would isolate them from their Croatian allies, satisfying the Croats by granting them trialist state status while the Slovenes would remain as they were and be given only some modest cultural autonomy. Receiving a delegation of Germans from Slovene territory on May 15, 1918, Emperor Karl spoke against a United Slovenia.

In order to put pressure on the opportunistic policy of the Croatian-Serbian coalition so it would choose the establishment of a common political representation for Slovenes, Croats, and Serbs, in Ljubljana on August 3, 1918, the Slovenes established the National Council for Slovenia and Istria as part of the future central National Co-mmittee of Slovenes, Croats, and Serbs in Zagreb. In September, this National Council for Slovenia, as the highest Slovene national representative body, began taking some governmental functions from the Austrian authorities still working such as collecting the financial means for its work and planning the future constitutional, legal, economic, and cultural development of Slovenia.

Prior to September 1918, people in Slovenia did not speak in public because of the censorship about the work of the Emigrant Yugoslav Committee (in which there were some second-class Slovene politicians) and the Corfu

Declaration that this Committee had issued in July 1917 together with the government of the Kingdom of Serbia and that had foreseen a unification of Hapsburg Southern Slavs with the Kingdom of Serbia. In September 1918, the constitutional-legal department of the National Council for Slovenia adopted a plan on the arrangement of the future Yugoslav state. It foresaw a federation of three units: Slovenia with Istria, Croatia and Slavonia with Vojvodina, and Bosnia and Herzegovina with Dalmatia. At a meeting of the department, the Slovene political leader Dr. Anton Korošec warned that this could eventually result in unification in the manner of the Corfu Declaration and the fourth unit would be Serbia. Of course, that was counting the chickens before they were hatched.

Only on October 6, 1918, was the National Parliament of Slovenes, Croats, and Serbs actually established in Zagreb with the consent of the Croatian-Serbian coalition, proclaiming itself as the highest political body of these nations.

On October 11th, in an audience with Emperor Karl, Dr. Korošec stressed that the Slovenes would not be satisfied with anything less than a free joint state with the Serbs and the Croats with Zagreb as its capital. The Slovenes had decided on such a radical decision in the first place because they had encountered complete misunderstanding and opposition from the ruling circles in Vienna and the Germans from the Slovene regions to Slovene national autonomy and a United Slovenia.

This German reaction diminished considerably the influence among the Slovenes of the conservative legitimist movement of Ivan Šušteršič, leader of the Slovene People's Party until the autumn of 1917, that was prepared to accept an autonomous Slovenia within the framework of Austria or at most to demand a Slovene-Croatian state.

On October 19th the National Parliament of Slovenes, Croats, and Serbs rejected Emperor Karl's manifesto on the reorganization of the Hapsburg Monarchy as a federation. On October 29th the Croatian Assembly in Zagreb and a huge popular rally in Ljubljana simultaneously proclaimed the establishment of the independent State of Slovenes, Croats, and Serbs.

IV. THE SLOVENES IN THE KINGDOM OF YUGOSLAVIA

14. The Dismemberment of Slovenia during the Transition from Austria to Yugoslavia

For a month after the proclamation of the independent State of Slovenes, Croats, and Serbs on October 29th, Slovenia actually lived an independent political life and administered itself, even though it considered itself a constituent part of the State of Slovenes, Croats, and Serbs and recognized its National Parliament as its highest government body.

On October 31st, the National Council for Slovenia was named the National Government of Slovenia, which the National Parliament in Zagreb confirmed immediately. With the exception of foreign affairs, which were reserved for the National Parliament in Zagreb, this government combined all the highest legislative and executive functions of the state. Through the work of the National Government in November, Slovene national self-determination was *ipso facto* expressed. On November 14th the National Government issued a decree on the transitional administration of Slovenia, its highest legal administrative act. Slovenia had to manage all its national affairs on its own, including the defence of its territory. It did not get any help from the National Parliament in Zagreb, and this presented serious difficulties. Already on October 31st, the German Provincial Government in Carinthia proclaimed the indivisibility of the province and its inclusion in the Republic of German Austria. On November 5th, the Italian army began to invade Slovene territory up to the line determined by the London Agreement and across it eastwards. On November 11th the Italian Army had reached Logatec where it was driven back by a division of soldiers of the National Government. However, the Italians retreated only as far as Planina, and Primorska and a great part of Notranjska were lost to Slovenia.

On November 1st, the Slovene Major Rudolf Maister took command of the garrison In Maribor and proclaimed Maribor and its surroundings Yugoslav possession, thus winning it for Slovenia. In Slovene Carinthia, however, Slovene military forces were too weak to resist the more numerous and better armed German *Heimwehr*, and by the end of 1918 the Slovene volunteer forces had been pushed out of Carinthia. Its destiny was left to the peace conference in Paris that in May 1919 ordered a plebiscite to be carried out in order to fix the boundaries of Carinthia. In October 1920, the plebiscite resulted in a negative outcome for Slovenia, and the Carinthian Slovenes remained in the Republic of Austria where they were systematically Germanized. The same happened to the Primorska Slovenes, who with the Treaty of Rapallo between the Kingdom of Slovenes, Croats, and Serbs and Italy in November 1920 finally fell to Italy. During the transition from Austria to Yugoslavia, the Slovene national body and territory were fatally dismembered. More than a quarter of the Slovenes and their territory were cut off from the mother country that joined the Yugoslav state. In the east, the small part of

Slovene territory in Porabje remained in Hungary.

In Slovenia, within the State of Slovenes, Croats, and Serbs, very intense political activity continued throughout November. Between November 16th and 18th, the Cultural Department of the National Council in Ljubljana discussed future cultural development and the status of the Slovene nation in the Yugoslav state. In spite of some neo-Illyrism and unitarian points of view, the opinion prevailed that the Slovene nation had to be preserved and must continue to develop as an independent national entity and that such state arrangements were necessary as to make auto-nomous development possible for the Slovenes.

The Cultural Department also passed a resolution on this matter signed by all members of the Department regardless their ideological and political orientation, but before it could be published, the Slovene Liberal Party that was striving for Yugoslav unitarism and a centralist state put pressure on its members in the Cultural Department to withdraw their signatures from the resolution. On November 23rd, the Liberal Party published the declaration of its cultural workers who according to the party's instructions expressed their support of Yugoslav national unitarism and immediate union with the Kingdom of Serbia.

The Catholic Slovene People's Party was opposed to such views and was not enthusiastic about the rapid and vague union of the Zagreb State of Slovenes, Croats, and Serbs with the Kingdom of Serbia. However, at a long and dramatic night session of the National

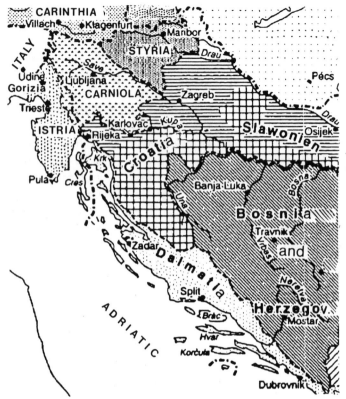

Territory of Slovenia before 1918

–·–·–		State borders after 1918
-----		State and administration borders before 1918

Austrian crown lands Carinthia, Carniola, Styria, Dalmatia, and Coastal Regions

Kingdom of Croatia and Slavonia (real union with Hungary)

Area of former military march

Kingdom of Hungary

Bosnia and Hercegovina (from 1878 under common administration of Austria and Hungary; to 1908 under Ottoman authority)

Parliament from November 24th to 25th in Zagreb, the supporters of immediate unconditional union prevailed, particularly the Croatian-Serbian coalition, the Dalmatian representatives, and the Serbs from Bosnia. In general, the most important and decisive factors for unification were the Serbs living on both banks of the Drina River who wanted to exploit this fortuitous moment to their advantage while the Kingdom of Serbia was a victorious state and an ally of the Entente. They wanted once and for all to solve the Serbian national question completely according to their own nationalist and centralist concept. The rest of the parties in the National Parliament were unable to oppose them with any effective instruments. The Kingdom of Serbia conceded equality to the National Parliament at the Geneva Conference from November 6th to 9th but abrogated it after a week.

Thus the parties opposed to a forced and vague form of unification, mainly the Slovene People's Party and the Croatian Party of Justice, showed too little resolve during the overnight meeting. They did not support the leader of the Croatian Peasant People's Party, Stjepan Radić, who was against such rapid unification with Serbia and demanded a guarantee of a high level of autonomy for Croatia in the future large Yugoslavia.

That night, overwhelmed by the enthusiasm for Yugoslavia, the National Parliament submitted to the advocates of the forced immediate unification which offered no guarantee for the autonomous positions of Croatia and Slovenia. The unification announced in Belgrade on December 1, 1918, established a unitarian centralist state according to Serbian concept called the Kingdom of Serbs, Croats, and Slovenes.

15. Political Life of the Slovenes in the Kingdom of Yugoslavia

One of the first steps of the newly established Kingdom of Serbs, Croats and Slovenes (renamed the Kingdom of Yugoslavia after King Alexander introduced a dictatorship on January 6, 1929) was to abolish the autonomous national governments in Croatia, Bosnia and Herzegovina, Dalmatia, and Slovenia in 1919. Belgrade replaced them with new official regional governments, causing great disappointment and dissatisfaction with the new state from its very beginning among the Croats and Slovenes.

In the temporary national representative body summoned in March 1919 primarily to prepare a new law for the elections to a constitutional assembly and several other common laws (for example, on agrarian reform), major disagreements began immediately.

Elections to the Constituent Assembly were delayed for nearly two years, until November 28, 1920. Before these elections, Slovenia had suffered two severe blows, the loss of the plebiscite in Carinthia and the Treaty of Rapallo, that severely struck the Slovenes and also influenced the outcome of the elections. More votes than usual were given to the parties striving for a unitarian and centralist Yugoslavia because people thought that only a strong and united state could protect the stricken Slovene nation. However, by the spring of 1921, the centralist pressure and the centralist unitarian constitutional plans, against which the Christian Social Slovene People's Party fought for the defense of Slovene autonomy, had returned the party to its previous political power, about two thirds of the electorate. It kept its power more or less unchanged until the collapse of the Kingdom of Yugoslavia.

The Vidovdan Constitution forced a unitarian and centralist arrangement on the Slovenes that was a major obstacle to national development. In the Constitutional Assembly, the centralist, primarily Serbian parties had a slight majority. However, at the time of its adoption, Slovene economic, social, political, and cultural life was so strongly developed in its own way that even the new state and civilizational framework could not repress, subjugate, or substantially change it. Originality, endurance, and considerable self-confidence were characteristic of the political life of the majority of the Slovene nation in the Kingdom of Yugoslavia.

Two fundamental problems dominated Slovene political life in the Kingdom of Yugoslavia. In the first place there were ideological and political extremes, rivalry, and sometimes even tense political battles between the Christian Social Slovene People's Party and the Liberal Party. The second problem was the struggle against state centralism and unitarism, that is, the struggle for the autonomy of Slovenia. The Slovene People's Party and the Liberal Party were already traditionally in opposition on almost all political issues. Their collaboration established during World War I reached its peak in the joint May Declaration, the National Council, and the endeavours for liberation under the Hapsburg Monarchy was only a short episode. Already in the earliest period of the new Yugoslav state, conflict regarding fundamental questions of Slovene political life flared up again. Diametrical differences in their attitudes to the national question became evident. The Liberals spoke in favour of Yugoslav national unity or unitarism and a corresponding centralist state formation. The Slovene People's Party was, at least until the end of 1920, for the development of Slovene national individuality and the autonomy of Slovenia.

Slovene Liberals were not unitarians and centralists just for competing political reasons against the Slovene People's Party but also because of erroneous sociological and cultural conceptions. In addition to this major national-political controversy, both central Slovene political parties (there were some minor parties including the Socialist Party, the Independent Liberal Peasant's Party, and the Communist Party) also opposed each other on economic, social, legal, political, educational, and cultural questions.

The Slovene People's Party strove for the protection of the farming population, the support of agricultural cooperatives, and lower farm taxes as well as the social protection of the working class and women's suffrage. The Liberals largely opposed these concepts and supported the greatest possible freedom for business. They favoured and encouraged the growth and power of financial capital.

Disputes between the two parties occurred especially in the educational and cultural sphere. It can be said that hardly anywhere in Europe such cultural battles raged as between the Liberal and Catholic Slovenes as when the Kingdom of Yugoslavia existed. The Catholics developed their comprehensive program to perfection at the fifth Catholic convention in 1923. Their guiding principle was the advancement of Christian ethnic principles in all spheres of public and private life. The Liberals could not oppose them with an equally radical program but sharply opposed the plans of the Slovene People's Party with individual articles in their newspaper and opposed their program in all spheres of power – whether in Belgrade or Ljubljana – in which they participated.

Both leading Slovene political parties had links with Belgrade. Each were at some time in the governing coalition and thus also governed in Slovenia for a certain period. After 1920, authority emanated from Belgrade, regardless of the actual political power and mandates of parties in the regions. From 1920 to 1927, the Slovene Liberals were in the Belgrade government and thus had a stronger position in Slovenia than they would have had considering the outcome of elections (they received around 20% of the vote). In 1927 the Slovene People's Party linked itself with Belgrade and took over all power in Slovenia. In the royal capital they realized that they would have to come to terms with the leading political force in Slovenia. From the national and political prospects of the Slovenes this move was a fatal turning point. The Slovene People's Party began to abandon its radical and principled national and political demands. In this respect it set sail in opportunistic waters that it did not know how to or could not leave until the end of the Kingdom of Yugoslav. So far, this policy has not been given thorough historical analysis. The question remains whether the party deserves condemnation because of its unprincipled behaviour or if with the political pragmatism embodied by party leader Dr. Anton Korošec it *ipso facto* established autonomy in Slovenia.

Only once after the major turning point in 1927 did the policy of the Slovene People's Party rise to its radical autonomous position. That was in December 1932 in the *Slovene Declaration*. At the time the party was in opposition to the unitarian dictatorial regime of King Alexander or rather illegal because it was forbidden. The *Slovene Declaration* stated that the Slovene nation was divided among four states: Yugoslavia, Italy, Austria, and Hungary. Its basic demand was to be united in one single political unit because only in this way could its general progress be assured. It was therefore the duty of the main part of the nation living in Yugoslavia to endeavour continuously for the realization of this ideal. All Slovenes in the Yugoslav state must fight for an independent position which would continually act as an drawing power for other parts of the nation living in other countries: "Thus we need national individuality, a name, a flag, ethnic community, financial independence, political and cultural freedom, a radical social legislature that must provide vital benefits, and the harmonious development of all necessary productive occupations, especially the farming and working classes. To achieve this goal it is necessary for Slovenes, Croats, and Serbs to create, after a free agreement and on a democratic basis, a state of autonomous units, one of which should be Slovenia." Supported by the Slovene Liberals, the regime forcibly arose against the authors of this declaration.

However, with the change of regime in 1935 and the taking office of Milan Stojadinović, the Slovene People's Party again linked itself with Great Serbia circles and the royal court and joined the ruling coalition, the Yugoslav Radical Community (Jugoslovanska radikalna zajednica). It quieted considerably its demands for the immediate formal establishment of an auto-nomous Slovenia but succeeded in informally maintaining autonomous Slovene authority in Slovenia.

From 1931-1932, processes of ideological and political differentiation concerning the national question began to appear in the two leading Slovene political parties. Leftist intellectual groups reproached the party leaderships with following an opportunistic policy harmful for the nation in Belgrade. Therefore a group of nationally conscious and active democratic intellectuals abandoned the unitarian and centralist Liberal Party and establis-hed their own paper, *Sodobnost* ("Contemporanei-ty"), around which a sort of national, liberal democratic political association was formed. At about the same time, the workers' wing of the Slovene People's Party left the party under the influence of the leftist Christian Socialists. They reproached the party for being lukewarm in the national policy toward Belgrade (the party's leaders responded to this accusation with the *Slovene Declaration*), but also for a too one-sided ideological orientation to the principles of the papal encyclical *Quadregesimo anno* and in practical policy for neglecting its support of the working class. After 1932, with their relatively strong trade union, the Christian Socialists became a considerable inde-pendent political force in Slovenia, interceding on behalf of socialism of the social democratic style considering, of course, the Christian ethos. After 1935 the Slovene Communists tried to attract and unite these smaller national democratic and Chris-tian socialist groups into the People's Front. In 1937 they established the seemingly organizationally independent Communist Party of Slovenia. They drafted an attractive democratic national political program that strove for a Slovene national republic within a federally reorganized Yugoslavia and won some sympathies and some allies among the Slovenes. However, acting on instructions from the Comintern in the autumn of 1939, the Communist Party of Slovenia abandoned the People's Front policy and attacked its former allies. Immediately before the war, political life in Slovenia was in total disarray.

16. The Slovenes under Italy, Austria, and Hungary

The national life of the Slovenes who remained in Austria and Hungary or came under Italy with the Treaty of Rapallo was extremely difficult. All three of these countries failed to honour their promises concerning the protection and free development of the Slovene minority agreed upon in the peace treaties. In these countries, therefore, the existence of the Slovene nation was threatened and all the work of the Slovenes was directed towards preservation so that political development among them did not develop normally.

As early as 1920, Fascism was in full swing in the border regions of Trieste and Istria, and one of its fundamental aims there was the struggle against the "foreign" Slovenes. In 1920, the Fascists burned down the Slovene National Center in Trieste, and after the Fascists came to power in October of 1922, conditions worsened for the Slovenes. In 1923, the Fascist authorities forbade Slovene in schools throughout Primorska, which they called Venezia Giulia, and also attempted to ban Slovene from all public life. Nationally-conscious Slovenes in the civil service such as teachers and railway clerks were transferred from Primorska deep into the interior of Italy or exiled to Yugoslavia. Under such pressure, many emigrated to Slovenia, to other parts of Europe, or to South America. The Italian state thus closed more than 150 Slovene primary and secondary schools. The Fascists Italianized Slovene surnames and place names. In 1926 Mussolini dissolved all political parties in the country and in 1928 the Slovene national organization *Edinost* ("Unity") in Trieste and Gorizia as well. Legal Slovene newspapers were suppressed, Slovene social, educational, cultural, and economic organizations were disbanded, all of which caused the Slovenes great material damage. All political dialogue between the Slovene minority and the Italian government was discontinued. The church was the only place where the Slovene language could still be used. From the mid-1920's, radical young nationalists established illegal organizations such as *Borba* ("Struggle") and TIGR (Trieste, Istria, Gorizia, Rijeka) for the struggle (including armed resistance) against the Fascists. From the end of the 1920's and throughout the 1930's, they carried out many armed actions against the Fascists and encouraged faith in annexation to Yugoslavia. This was the first armed anti-Fascism movement in Europe, and the Fascist regime responded to this activity with drastic punishments.

Until 1933, Carinthian Slovenes in Austria lived in a formal democracy, although the Austrian Republic also followed a denationalizing policy against them using all kinds of economic, social, moral, and political pressures. For the government, Slovenes as such, were considered suspicious, especially those who had voted for Yugoslavia in the 1920 plebiscite. The results of this German pressure were reflected in the census reports: in 1910 Slovenes in Carinthia numbered 82,000, but in 1923 only 39,000. Such a decline could not be the result of normal demographic development. In 1927, the Slovenes intensified their efforts to achieve national autonomy, but German parties rejected this move. From 1921, Carinthian Slovenes united in a political and economic association of Carinthian Slovenes. In the association, whose members were predominantly farmers, Catholic political influence dominated. The principal aim of the association was to maintain Slovene land ownership, to develop national culture and education on Catholic foundations, and to see to all fields of Slovene economy. In 1934, the new authoritarian Catholic regime dissolved the Slovene Political and Economic Association. The only organization left to the Slovenes was the Catholic Slovene Cultural Union led by Dr. Jožko Tischler.

In 1938, after the German Nazis had incorporated Austria in the Third Reich, pressure on Carinthian Slovenes was increased still further with the aim of Germanizing Carinthia as soon as possible. The Slovenes, of course, continued their defiance.

With the 1920 Treaty of Trianon, Slovene Porabje (the Raba River region) with its center at Monošter still remained within the framework of the Hungarian state. In the period between the two World Wars, Hungary did not provide a Slovene primary school but systematically Hungarianized them. This was done in the belief that the Porabje Slovenes were Wends and that Wends also lived in Slovenia as a special Germanic nation descended from the Vandals. In spite of everything, some 4000 Slovenes remained in Porabje villages in the postwar period.

17. Economic, Social, and Cultural Development in Slovenia between the World Wars

In spite of its strong political centralism and Serbian hegemony, the first Yugoslavia undoubtedly made it possible for the Slovenes to progress economically and culturally and thus to strengthen their national existence. Upon union with Yugoslavia, the Slovenes numbered almost one million and some 350,000 lived outside Yugoslav borders in Italy and Austria), while before the occupation in 1941 the Slovene population in Yugoslavia was estimated to number around 1,150,000. Due to the nationalizing pressures, the demographic development of the Slovene nation in Austria and Italy was curtailed and the number of Slovenes decreased.

Economically, the Slovenes in Yugoslavia developed quickly. In both decades, the rapid industrialization of the country was evident, although there was minor stagnation during the economic crisis between 1930 and 1934. Along with the older surviving ironworking and coal mining industries, primarily the manufacture of consumer goods grew, finding grateful markets in the underdeveloped southern parts of Yugoslavia. In Slovenia, a number of new large textile plants developed and took their place alongside older ones. Metal processing and chemical industries developed, and the leather and paper industries expanded. Parallel with this development, considerable change occurred in the social structure, and by 1941 only 55% of the population was engaged in agriculture. In spite of its intensive development, however, industry could not absorb all the redundant work force from the countryside, and this presented a major social problem. Agriculture was dominated by small landowners who were constantly on the margin of existence.

In the twenty years of development, Slovene education and culture made the greatest advance.

In the new Yugoslav state, all schools became Slovene and their numbers increased, especially the number of primary, secondary, and polytechnical schools. In 1919, the Slovenes acquired their first university in Ljubljana, which gave the younger generation the cultural and scientific education so important for national existence. Several important cultural and scientific institutions were also established: the National Museum, the National Gallery, the Slovene National Theatre, Radio Ljubljana (1928), and the Academy of Sciences and Arts (1938). Cultural, artistic, and scientific creativity flourished, and in these spheres Slovenes strove to match the achievements of their Central European neighbours.

Much of the effort of the deliberate educational and cultural policy went toward eliminating the dominant and very powerful German influence and replacing it with the French influence with some success. It is hard to find any kind of cultural influence from Belgrade, although there was some from Zagreb. All this progress considerably strengthened Slovene national awareness, and with it criticism grew regarding centralist Yugoslavia as well as the resolve to achieve federative status within it.

V. THE SLOVENES IN WORLD WAR II AND IN THE FEDERAL SOCIALIST YUGOSLAVIA

18. The Occupation and Dismemberment of Slovenia during World War II

Yugoslavia avoided becoming entangled in the war for a year and a half. In the spring of 1941, however, under pressure from Germany and Italy, it was forced to join the Triple Alliance. The British neither wanted to nor could guarantee effective help from the sea or by land from Greece. Immediately after Yugoslavia had joined the Triple Alliance, the British organized a military coup in Yugoslavia, thus removing the Regent Prince Pavel and the existing government. For this reason, Hitler decided to attack Yugoslavia. At the same time, he wanted to secure transportation routes for his attack on Greece and secure his flank for the attack on the Soviet Union he had already planned. His decision to attack was easily made as his ally Mussolini had continually urged him to attack and dismember Yugoslavia. After the onslaught of the German army on April 6th, the Yugoslav Army collapsed in little over a week. On April 10th, the pro-Fascist Croatian nationalists, the *Ustashi*, proclaimed all the territory of Croatia and Bosnia and Herzegovina the Independent State of Croatia. Originating as a part of the occupational system, this state became a German-Italian protectorate. Slovenia was thus completely cut off from the rest of Yugoslavia and divided among the three invaders who occupied it completely by the 11th of April. The

German Third Reich took for itself Štajerska and Gorenjska, the Hungarians took part of Prekmurje, and the Italians occupied Notranjska, Dolenjska, and Ljubljana. After the occupation, all three occupiers violated international law and simply annexed Slovene territory, introducing their political and legal systems. The Italians were the fastest to do so, and on May 3rd they annexed the newly occupied Slovene territories to Italy as the Ljubljana Province. The Hungarians proclaimed annexation in December 1941. For various reasons the Germans postponed the official legal annexation of Slovene regions, although in fact they included them in their state and political system so that the highest authorities in the provinces became the *Gauleiters* of Styria and Carinthia who at the same time became heads of the civil administration for Štajerska and Gorenjska. The ultimate aim of all three occupiers was to destroy the Slovenes as a nation, a goal both Hitler and Mussolini declared publicly. They differed only in their methods of denationalization and the time they allotted to achieve this aim. Each of the occupiers was convinced that the occupied Slovene territory would be transformed into his own province.

For tactical and political reasons the Italian regime in the Ljubljana Province showed the Slovenes a friendly face and allowed them their cultural autonomy and their own administration at the lower levels. Both the German and Hungarian occupiers at once began the repression of the Slovenes with all their force, immediately abolishing Slovene education, Slovene administration, and all national

SLOVENIA 1941-1945

▪-▪-▪	State borders before the division of Yugoslavia
----	Border lines after the division
▪--▪--▪	German - Italian Demarcation Line
▫	Territory of the Independent State of Croatia
▨	Territories annexed by Hungary
▦	Territories annexed by Germany
▩	Territories annexed by Italy

organizations. The Germans immediately began to execute their ruthless, previously prepared plan of ethnic cleansing: the deportation of all the Slovene intelligentsia and nationally-conscious population, including the clergy. Their intention was to deport a quarter of the population from Štajerska and Gorenjska and the remainder were to be completely Germanized within a few years. Slovene intelligentsia were deported to Serbia and Croatia and the rural population to the Reich.

As High Commissioner of the Ljubljana Province, the Italian occupier selected the Fascist Emilio Grazioli, who had previously advanced his career by persecuting the Primorska Slovenes.

The difference between the Italian and German occupation was that the Italians summoned the Slovenes and their organizations to cooperate with the Italian authorities, a course the Germans rejected because they wanted to immediately erase any trace of the Slovene identity in their occupied territories. For the occupied population, the Italian policy was tempting, particularly as the Ljubljana Province had accepted 20,000 refugees from Štajerska. However, every observant Slovene knew from the experience of the Primorska Slovenes what Slovenes in the Ljubljana Province could expect.

19. The National Liberation Struggle and the Civil War

On the whole the Slovene population rejected the occupation, and only the small German minority in Štajerska welcomed it. Prior to the beginning of the occupation there were no Fascist political groups or movements in Slovenia that would welcome the occupation for ideological motives and would have been prepared in advance to collaborate with the occupier. The Slovenes recoiled and were disposed to wait and see how the political and military situation would develop; this attitude was based on the belief that the Western democracies would be victorious and that Yugoslavia would rise up again with a free United Slovenia. But among certain people the conviction prevailed that it was necessary to begin immediate armed resistance against the occupier and thus win a place in the new postwar democratic world through their own struggle.

In the first days of the occupation, the existing political elite that remained in the Ljubljana Province were largely inclined to attempt to find some *modus vivendi* with the occupier, privately still recognizing the continued authority of the Yugoslav government in exile in London and the Slovene deputies in it, while at home they leaned on their former supporters. In the Ljubljana Province they accepted a functional collaboration with the Italian occupier, justifying this policy by saying they were thus best protecting the Slovene population and offering shelter to many Slovene refugees from German occupied areas.

This functional collaboration with the Italian occupier in the Ljubljana Province (the Germans in Štajerska and the Italians in Primorska rejected such collaboration), for example, joining the advisory committee of the High Commissariat, being overly loyal and grateful in their statements to the Italian State and Mussolini drew reproach and moral objections from the Allies and even more from their political adversaries at home. In their political and strategic considerations, the former ruling elite were not prepared to risk immediate active and armed resistance against the occupier at the risk of victims, as was the case in some European countries although in the history of European civilization such actions have always brought moral glory and political capital.

Things were different with some other levels of the Slovene population, especially among the youth, a large part of the Slovene intelligentsia, and in certain districts also among the farmers. From the very beginning they were prepared for any form of resistance against the occupier. This inclination was evident in some smaller political groups from the leftist National Democrats (the *Sokoli* or "Falcons") and the leftist Catholic Christian Socialists to the Communists, who before the war had already opposed the policies of the two bourgeois parties, the Clericals and the Liberals. The Communists also had a different political philosophy, a philosophy that included revolutionary and armed action. Three weeks after the occupation they realized that it would be possible to organize a mass resistance movement in Slovenia through which they could achieve not only national liberation but also defeat their old political adversaries in their own nation, that is, the old political elite.

The Anti-imperialist Front established at the end of April that after the German attack on the Soviet Union was renamed the Liberation Front appealed to Slovenes to immediately start armed resistance against the occupier, emphasizing its aim was to fight for the liberation of the occupied Slovene nation, to form a free United Slovenia that would independently decide on its future fate and its political links. Direct action associated with the prospect of a revolutionary break with the previous order that had satisfied hardly anyone attracted the youth and the left wing groups. Within a few months, the Liberation Front and the first partisan units actually enjoyed at least the passive support of the wider strata of society. It also became increasingly clear that in this campaign the Communist Party of Slovenia had the decisive word (the political secretary of the Liberation Front was the Communist Boris Kidrič).

Two important items among the September resolutions of the High Plenum of the Liberation Front were firstly that the Liberation Front claimed for itself the exclusive right to represent the nation during the war against the occupier and that any organizing of Slovenes outside the framework of the Liberation Front was harmful to the nation and treacherous, and secondly that the Liberation Front would place Slovene partisan units under the joint command of the Yugoslav partisan army. The first item revealed the exclusive character of the Liberation Front and its monopolistic ambition directed against political rivals, while the second item displayed its involvement in the pan-Yugoslav resistance movement under the leadership of the Communist Party of Yugoslavia and its Secretary General Josip Broz Tito.

This clearly declared orientation of the Liberation Front and its early practice of settling accounts with its political enemies frightened its opponents among the old political elite. In the autumn of 1941, they began a sharp propaganda campaign in the press and by word of mouth against the Liberation Front, attempted to label the armed resistance, which already shown results, adventurism that provoked the occupier and caused unnecessarily large numbers of victims. They reproached the Liberation Front for being under the influence of the Communists and for beginning a revolution. The opinion of the old political elite was shared by the conservative Bishop Rožman of Ljubljana, who was baffled by these extremely complicated events.

The Liberation Front maintained again and again that it did not want a revolution and that it wanted to settle all domestic social, and political problems only after the occupier had been driven out, its primary and basic task, but in reality it attempted through direct measures to strengthen its political position in the nation and assure power for itself before the end of the war.

Among the old political elite, fear and hatred of Communism overruled all other political reasons and considerations. The prewar ideological indoctrination was the real foundation of the severe and irreconcilable polarization among the Slovenes. At the beginning of 1942, the old elite began to organize opposition against the Communists and thus also against the Liberation Front. At the beginning, with the establishment of the Slovene Covenant, this was still their independent action without the occupier. Some people in the anti-Communist camp felt threatened by the major partisan successes in the spring of 1942 and by the revolutionary Communist excesses in the field. Being too weak themselves, they began to seek help from the occupiers, thus slipping into collaboration with them against their own countrymen in the Liberation Front. The anti-revolutionary camp thus entered a blind alley politically or military and stepped out of the context of World War II, which was a confrontation between democracy and aggressive totalitarian Nazi Fascism. In addition to the liberation war against the occupier, in part of Slovene territory, that is, in the Ljubljana Province, a civil war also erupted among the Slovenes themselves in the spring of 1942. In the greater part of Slovenia, in Štajerska, Primorska, and largely in Gorenjska, there was no civil war, but the developments in the central Slovene region and their result influenced all of Slovenia at the end of the war. From the end of 1941, Slovene partisans fought countless battles with the occupier over the whole Slovene territory, suffering many defeats and terrible casualties but also achieving great successes. By the summer of 1942, the Slovene partisans were organized into numerous mobile shock brigades. Two large shock brigades from the Ljubljana Province where the partisan army was the strongest succeeded in advancing across the German border into Štajerska to help the Štajerska partisans who were in a difficult situation under the German occupier. Upon the capitulation of Italy in September 1943, the Slovene partisan army disarmed three Italian divisions in the territory of the Ljubljana Province and almost completely smashed the anti-Communist militia, the armed force of its collaborating domestic political enemies. At the end of 1943, the Slovene partisan army was acknowledged to be an Allied military force as part of the Yugoslav partisan army.

In the autumn of 1941, the Liberation Front had established the Slovene National Liberation Committee as the highest representative body of the Slovene nation as well as subordinate committees throughout Slovene territory. These were usually the local committees of the Liberation Front. From its foundation, the Slovene National Committee passed various resolutions, decisions, and declarations based on the right of the Slovene nation to self-determination and sovereignty regarding the position of the Slovene nation in course of the Liberation War, its relationship with the former Yugoslav state and its neighbours, and boundary issues. It strove for a sovereign Slovene national status or an independent United Slovenia with the status of a republic within the framework of a future Yugoslav Federation. It demanded that the future United Slovenia include all the ethnic territory that had been Slovene before the process of forceful and systematic imperialist denationalizing pressure had begun. Trieste would therefore also belong to a United Slovenia.

From October 1 to October 3, 1943, the Liberation Front convened a major assembly of 572 delegates of the Slovene nation in Kočevje that elected 120 members to the Slovene National Liberation Committee. On the principle of national self-determination, the Kočevje Assembly decided to include the free Slovenia, including Primorska, in the new Federal Yugoslavia that had been forming since the first session of the Anti-Fascist Parliament of the

National Liberation of Yugoslavia (AVNOJ) in Bihać in November 1942. At the second session of AVNOJ held in Jajce in November 1943, which a Slovene delegation attended, AVNOJ proclaimed itself the highest legislative body of the New Federal Yugoslavia and established its Liberation Government. Under pressure from the major anti-Fascist allies, an agreement was reached between the exiled Royal Government in London and the AVNOJ Government in the spring of 1944. The agreement was signed on the island of Vis by their presidents Dr. Ivan Šubašič and Josip Broz Tito. The agreement was recognized by the Allies and thus the Slovene Liberation Front became an internationally recognized political force and authority. With this move, the Allies finally buried all hopes of the Slovene counterrevolution and its armed formation, the Slovene Home Guard (*Domobranci*). The leadership of the Slovene counterrevolution even received an order from London to come to an agreement with the Liberation Front and for the Home Guard units by all means to stop collaborating with the Germans. Unfortunately, no agreement was reached and at the end of the war the counterrevolutionary camp was consequently left out of decisions regarding the new political life in Slovenia. After the end of the war, the armed supporters of the counterrevolution and collaboration met with tragedy. The British, to whom they had turned for help, surrendered the members of the Slovene Home Guard to the Slovene partisans or the Yugoslav Army and the majority were executed.

The Slovene partisan army that had cooperated militarily with the Allies, together with the Yugoslav army, liberated all Slovene ethnic territory. The governing of Slovenia was taken over by the Liberation Front that politically was completely dominated by the Communists. The result of the partisans' national liberation struggle was outwardly the creation of a United Slovenia, but internally it was the formation of a Slovene republic within the Yugoslav Federation with the right to self-determination, including the right to secede.

20. United Slovenia at the End of the War and at the Paris Peace Conference

Following the end of the war in the spring of 1945, the Free United Slovenia was only a short-lived reality. Faced with an ultimatum from the Anglo-American command, Yugoslav forces including the Slovene partisans had to begin withdrawing from Carinthia on May 19, 1945, and relinquish authority to the Anglo-American forces and the Austrians. On June 12th the Yugoslav Army also had to withdraw from Trieste and its surroundings as far as the line dictated by General Morgan, Chief of Staff of the Anglo-American forces in the Mediterranean. The Yugoslav Army and the Slovene authorities retained liberated Primorska as far as the Morgan Line, including access to the Adriatic Sea at Koper. So far, historians not given a satisfactory explanation of what led the Allies to impose the ultimatum on their Yugoslav ally so that it had to withdraw from the borders of Slovene ethnic territory. Some believe the ultimatum was the result of the decision by the Yugoslav leadership to sign the friendship agreement with the Soviet Union on April 14, 1945, that enraged the British and the Americans. For historians, the question also remains open as to why Tito and the Yugoslav Army so quickly accepted this ultimatum and did not risk attempting a military resistance to the ultimatum.

After this retreat, the federal leadership headed by Tito and the leadership of the Liberation Front were quite confident and maintained it would be possible to secure Slovenia its rightful borders at a peace conference where Yugoslavia and Slovenia would be supported by the whole freedom-loving world, above all by their friend the Soviet Union.

At the peace conference which was held from July to October 1946, these hopes were unfortunately dashed. It was soon decided that the border to Austria would remain unchanged, which meant that the Carinthian Slovenes would remain cut off from the mother nation in Slovenia.

Negotiations over the western border with Italy lasted much longer. The Yugoslav delegation led by Foreign Minister Edvard Kardelj, a Slovene, laid claim to the entire Slovene ethnic territory including Trieste, which the Yugoslav state would allow the status of free city in a union with Yugoslavia. This claim was opposed by the Allies who did not want to see the Yugoslav Army, an ally of the Soviet Red Army, in Trieste. The Cold War had begun.

While the peace conference lasted, many demonstrations were organized in Primorska at which people demanded its annexation to Yugoslavia under the slogan *Tujega nočemo, svojega ne damo* ("We do not want what is not ours nor will we give away what is ours").The peace conference agreed to a French proposal as a kind of compromise solution according to which Slovene Venetia, Resia, Val Canale, and Gorizia were ceded to Italy while Yugoslavia got the remainder of Primorska, Istria with Rijeka, and all the Adriatic islands with Zadar. From the Trieste, Koper, and Buje regions they created the Free Trieste Territory that was divided into Zone A (Trieste and its surroundings) under Anglo-American administration and Zone B (the Koper and Buje regions) under Yugoslav administration. The Free Trieste Territory was to be a small autonomous state under the auspices of the United Nations administered by a governor and an elected assembly. The Yugoslav delegation did not want to accept such a demarcation and left the peace conference in protest. In February 1947, under pressure from the great powers, Yugoslavia signed the peace treaty, still hoping secretly that on some other favourable occasion it would be able to annex even the Free Trieste Territory. The Slovenes in particular hoped this wish would be realized. The Free Trieste Territory became one of the first crisis points in Europe and remained so until Cold War tensions began to relax in 1954.

At the end of 1945, the Slovene right to self-determination within the framework of the Democratic Federal Republic of Yugoslavia was at risk. In the constitution proposed by the Constitutional Assembly (the Assembly had been elected on November 14, 1945, and on November 29th had proclaimed the Democratic Federal Yugoslavia a republic) the right of individual nations to self-determination and secession was originally left out. At the demand of the Slovenes led by Edvard Kardelj, this right which derived from the voluntary incorporation of the Slovenes in the Federal Yugoslavia in the autumn of 1943 and from the AVNOJ declaration in the spring of 1944 was written into the Yugoslav Constitution adopted in January 1946. However, already at the very beginnings of the Federal Yugoslavia it was clear that the Serb nation and its leadership did not understand or accept a federalism based on the genuine internal sovereignty of the nations and their republics. This was the basic background for all the future development of Slovenia within the federal Yugoslavia.

21. Slovene Development in the Communist Administered State System

From liberation onwards, development in Slovenia proceeded according to laws passed by the central government in Belgrade that were largely made to measure for the Serbian majority population that lived in three republics: Serbia, Bosnia and Herzegovina, and Croatia. It was given its basic social and political character by a Communist regime trying almost entirely to copy the Bolshevist system of the Soviet Union with a single Communist Party totally governing all public life. This arose from the position of the monolithic Marxist-Leninist ideology and voluntarism in the development of social and economic structures. This system had a very narrow Bolshevist class concept of democracy that in the case of Yugoslavia and Slovenia additional legitimized itself by emphasizing its role in the anti-Fascist struggle and in the victory over the occupier and in establishing a "people's democracy."

While in many respects from the social and economic viewpoint, Federal Yugoslavia was more centralist than the Kingdom of Yugoslavia for these reasons, Slovenia and the other republics lived an autonomous educational and cultural life. In addition, however, due to its greater development and more qualified work force, Slovenia developed economically much faster even within the unified Yugoslav social and economic system and its GDP and national income were far above the average.

A decade and a half after liberation, Slovenia was developing economically very rapidly. In the desire to further speed development, the development of industry in particular was accelerated at the expense of agriculture to create in accordance with Bolshevist thought a more numerous working class, the bearers of socialism. The collectivization of almost all means of productions was accomplished. Only small and medium farm properties remained in private hands. The consequence of such development was fundamental demographic restructuring and major urbanization.

Within two years after the war, the postwar restoration was finished and then began the first five-year plan to build up socialism following the model of the Soviet Union. After its first five years of existence, the new state experienced a great shock. In the spring of 1948 there was a political rift between Yugoslavia and the Soviet Union that had little to do with ideology or the system but was a matter of the affirmation of Yugoslavia's state sovereignty and emancipation. The leadership of the Yugoslav Communists under Tito displayed considerable unity and succeeded in defying the pressure of Stalin and all the European Communist parties (Cominform). Some members of the Communist Party opposed the break with the Soviet Union, but in all the republics their number was smallest in Slovenia.

The conflict and break with the Soviet Union did not slow the development of socialist structures in Yugoslavia, and after 1950 Slovenia got a special Yugoslav configuration: "workers' self-management." Over the years, workers' self-management asserted itself as the basic social and political structure of Yugoslavia. The Slovene Communists headed by Edvard Kardelj were at the forefront of the theoretical and practical development of self-management socialism.

For many years Slovene Communists did not raise the Slovene national question in the internal Yugoslav plan, particularly as the conviction prevailed that the National Liberation struggle and the socialist revolution had resolved this question in the best possible way. In reality, however, Slovenes encountered the painful question of the Slovene minority in Zone A of the Free Trieste Territory, in Italy, and in Carinthia in Austria. In the autumn of 1953, the Anglo-American authorities announced that they would hand control of Zone A to Italy. Yugoslavia protested sharply. The brief Trieste Crisis followed, and a year later the Free Trieste Territory was abolished. In accordance with the

London Memorandum, Zone A of the Free Trieste Territory was given to Italy while Zone B remained under Yugoslav authority. The Slovenes retained their access to the Adriatic at Koper. The provisional London Memorandum lasted until 1975 when Italy and the Socialist Federal Republic of Yugoslavia signed an international agreement in Ossimo that confirmed the existing borders. A year after the London Memorandum was signed, the Slovenes were forced to surrender their hopes for United Slovenia in Carinthia as well. On May 15, 1955, the Belvedere Treaty or Austrian State Treaty on the restoration of a democratic and independent Austria was signed. This treaty signed by Austria and Yugoslavia along with the great powers guaranteed Austria its 1938 boundaries. However, Article 7 of the treaty listed a number of provisions concerning the protection of the Slovene minority in Austria and the right of Yugoslavia to watch over the implementation of this Austrian obligation.

Even today, however, the two Slovene minority communities in Italy and Austria do not enjoy all the minority rights that the Council of Europe demands and that the Italian and Hungarian minorities in Slovenia enjoy. Owing to the rapid economic and other civilizational changes tending toward the ever-increasing urbanization of populations, the number of members of the Slovene minorities in Austria and Italy is still decreasing.

22. The Flourishing of Workers' and Social Self-Management (1955-1970)

For the economy, the second half of the 1950's meant rapid growth in the physical extent of industrial production and the introduction of self-management in industrial enterprises. The Communist Party, now called the League of Communists, kept power firmly in its hands although it announced that it would withdraw from direct political administration. This position was most emphatically declared at the 7th Congress of the League of Communists of Yugoslavia held in Ljubljana in April 1958. The program adopted was an innovation in the development of the international Communist movement since it was the first to admit the reformist evolutional development of capitalist society into socialism and advocate the concept of a self-managing workers' democracy; however, it still reserved the decisive ideological and political role derived from Leninist ideology for the League of Communists. In the development of this program a decisive role was played by the Slovene Edvard Kardelj, who also formulated the position of the League of Communists toward the national question in opposition to the unitarian and centralist views of some Serbian and Montenegrin Communists.

At the beginning of the 1960's, the rapid industrial growth stopped and the Yugoslav state was faced with its first major economic crisis: too little accumulation of capital, structural discrepancies in industrial production, too slow modernization, too low productivity, and the lagging behind of development in agriculture.

The state began to increase its investment in agriculture, first in state-owned properties and later in privately-owned farms as well.

In 1963, Yugoslavia adopted a new constitution which broadly introduced self-management in all spheres of life. Government organs were composed as a kind of corporate representation of various fields of work. This constitution also allotted great importance to larger municipalities that were to become the basic social cells for the comprehensive development of socialist structures. The Assembly of Nations of the Federal Parliament was constitutionally abolished and with it every guarantee of a genuine federal system. With the economic reforms in the middle of the 1960's, the League of Communists attempted to introduce more marketing, rational management, and economizing. It allowed the redundant work force to go to Western Europe to work, thereby unburdening the labour market and at the same time drawing much needed foreign currency sent by migrant workers into the country, thus improving the standard of living of the population. National borders were completely open, passports were easy to obtain, and visas were no longer required by most foreign countries.

In 1966, the forces within the League of Communists of Yugoslavia headed by Aleksander Ranković, were defeated, and the republics received greater authority in the sphere of economic development. This resulted in a rise in the power of republic parties and the administrative political elite who advocated increasing the power and competence of the republics at the expense of the center. In some republics (Slovenia, Croatia, Serbia) this elite enabled the spread of a mercantile marketing mentality and more liberal views within the League of Communists of Yugoslavia. Slovenia's Prime Minister Stane Kavčič strove to restructure the Slovene economy by developing more modern industries such as electronics, banking, and service activities while opening Slovenia to Europe and increasing links with it. Because of his views concerning development, after 1969 the federal government leadership and the more conservative Slovene Communists thwarted his political efforts during the following two years. Similarly, by means of party discipline, liberal streams within the League of Communists in Slovenia and in other republics that were striving for a more market-oriented economy and more pronounced republic and ethnic sovereignty were also foiled.

23. The Crisis of Self-management and Ethnic Relations in Yugoslavia

Events at the beginning of the 1970's with the purging of "nationalists" and "liberals" from party ranks convinced the party and government leadership headed by Tito, Kardelj, and Bakarić that it was necessary to give greater autonomy to the nations and republics in the federation. This was reflected in the new constitution of 1974, which established a genuine federal system with elements of confederation. The social economic basis of this constitution was based on the "direct democracy of freely united producers," a beautiful humanist utopia that could never be realized. While the whole political system was conceived as a direct democracy with a delegate system, in practice it could never completely work. This system did not do away with the ever growing economic difficulties, and in a federal government with an ever increasing bureaucracy, no concrete common economic system could ever be agreed upon. All the republics were dissatisfied with the functioning of the federation and blamed each other as the differences between them became ever larger. Yugoslavia rapidly began to run up debts to the West.

After the defeat of party liberalism, Slovenia lived for a good decade and a half under a relatively conservative and rigid communist regime which in its unrealistic assessment of the direction and possibilities of development made some major errors concerning economic development. In spite of all the erroneous developmental decisions, a visible process of economic modernization continued in Slovenia. Being more developed, Slovenia had a constant advantage over other parts of Yugoslavia. It produced an approximately two and a half times higher GDP and national income than the Yugoslav average, and Slovene consumer goods were in great demand on the Yugoslav market. At the beginning of the 1980's, with only 8.3% of the population of Yugoslavia, Slovenia was producing up to 18% of the Yugoslav GDP and up to 25% of Yugoslavia's total export. Some 33% of all Yugoslav goods exported to Western markets were made in Slovenia. All this, however, did not eliminate Slovenia's problems of overemployment and low productivity that certainly made its goods competitive on the Yugoslav market but not on the European market. Slovene agriculture struggled with the same problem, because the part-time production of crops on small dispersed farms was far too expensive and adequate only for the farmers' own needs. Still enjoying a relatively good standard of living, however, the Slovenes developed a sense for better management while at the same time leaning toward asserting greater Slovene self-confidence and achieving an appropriate position within Yugoslavia with their economic power.

With the death of the historical leaders of the revolution and socialist development (Tito, Kardelj, Bakarić) who had succeeded in controlling the political situation in Yugoslavia with the instruments of party policies, a very important subjective factor was lost. In the first half of the 1980's, sharp interethnic and interrepublic conflicts appeared, aggravated by the economic crisis. Interethnic conflict first erupted in Kosovo between the Serbs and the Albanians, and possibly this was the reason that in the middle of the 1980's Serb nationalism took the offensive against the 1974 Yugoslav constitution. It opposed the constitution's confederative scheme and proposed the greater centralization and unity of the state in the economic and even cultural fields (e.g., a uniform core school curriculum for all of Yugoslavia).

The first in Slovenia to oppose the experiment of cultural and educational unification of the state were the writers and educators in 1985. The 1986 memorandum of the Serbian

Academy of Sciences openly brought forward the nationalist Great Serbia program and its principle of "all Serbs in one state" heralded the coming pressure on all the federal units where ethnic Serbs lived alongside majority non-Serbian populations. This was also followed by economic measures directed against Slovenia.

This stirred wide opposition in Slovenia, not only in cultural circles but in some economic circles as well. Slovenia felt economically strong and was no long prepared to bow to a centralism that did not promise modernization, development, or closeness to the European Union. In this situation, the Slovene Communists trapped in the common Yugoslav League of Communists could not offer a way out of the crisis. Their historical role was exhausted.

VI. THE DISSOLUTION OF YUGOSLAVIA AND THE ESTABLISHMENT OF THE INDEPENDENT REPUBLIC OF SLOVENIA

24. Origin of the Anti-Communist Opposition and Its Victory in the 1987-1990 Elections

In the spring of 1987, a group of intellectuals (predominantly anti-Communist liberals and Catholics) associated with the magazine *Nova revija* ("New Review") published articles outlining a Slovene national program in which they demanded the introduction of political pluralism, democracy, a market economy, and independence for Slovenia (in an eventual Yugoslav confederation). Everywhere in Yugoslavia such views encountered strong opposition and condemnation. After brief opposition, the new liberal and predominantly social democratic leadership of the Slovene Communists, since 1986 led by Milan Kučan, decided to drop their opposition, and many Communists began to associate themselves with the demands published in *Nova revija*.

In the spring of 1988, the Belgrade central government in which the leader of the Serbian Communists Slobodan Milošević had increasing influence decided to put pressure on the Slovenes as the supporters of modernization, democratiza-tion, and the demands for confederation and reduce them to obedience as an example. It arrested a group of four young Slovenes headed by Janez Janša and accused them of working against the Yugoslav Army. It staged a show trial against them before a military court in Ljubljana in the Serbian language instead of Slovene. However, the trial had exactly the opposite effect on the Slovene public than Belgrade had intended. It increased the obstinate will of the Slovenes and strongly united them behind the program to achieve democratization, political pluralism, and national independence. In the summer, Milan Kučan, the leader of the Slovene League of Communists, declared that the Slovene nation could not respect a state that did not respect the Slovene language. The President of the Presidency of Slovenia Janez Stanovnik added that in future Slovenes would think, make decisions, and work in Slovene.

In the autumn of 1988, the central government and the Serbs succeeded for the last time in depriving other nations of some of their sovereign rights through constitutional amendments.

The year 1989 brought continuing tension in relations between Slovenia and the federal government that was in the hands of the Serbs during which Slovenia displayed its will and strength. In February, a public meeting in the Cankarjev dom Congress Center in Ljubljana organized jointly by the Slovene Government and the opposition parties condemned the political and police violence of the Serbian authorities in Kosovo and called for peace and coexistence. From the beginning of the year, new political parties or "unions" as they had to be called according to the law were being formed in Slovenia: the Democratic Union of Slovenia, the Social Democratic Union, the Farmers' Union, and finally the Christian

Democratic Union. In May, at a large rally on Kongresni trg square in Ljubljana, the Slovene opposition parties adopted the "May Declaration" for "a sovereign state of the Slovene nation" that would "as a sovereign state decide independently on its links with South Slav and other nations within the framework of a renewed Europe" and would "be based on respect for human rights, freedom, and democracy and would also include political pluralism and the spiritual and material welfare of the citizens of Slovenia."

In spite of severe pressure and threats from Belgrade, the Slovene Parliament adopted amendments to the Slovene Constitution in September 1989 through which the Republic of Slovenia reclaimed the sovereign national rights it had ceded at the foundation of the Yugoslav Federation in 1943. This significant action was taken by a Slovene Parliament still composed of members elected through the one-party Communist system. This decisive session of the Slovene Parliament was attended by Janez Drnovšek, President of the Presidency of the Socialist Federal Republic of Yugoslavia, the first Slovene in such an important office to show solidarity with the independent decision of the Slovene republic. All this is a convincing indicator of how strongly anchored the attitude of the Slovenes was in the autumn of 1989 that the Slovene nation and its government had to shake off the influence of the less progressive and culturally quite different republics and acquire the actual right to decide independently on its continuing national development in the economic, political, and cultural fields. On this point, the supporters of socialist government and their antisocialist opposition were united: they differed only in their views on how quickly and in what form independence should be attained. In the hope of reaching an agreement with the central government and the Serbs, the "socialist" government proposed an asymmetrical federation, while the opposition demanded confederation as a minimum. The two sides also differed in their views concerning the structure of Slovenia's internal political life. The government still favoured some kind of democratized and pluralized single "Socialist Union," while the democratic opposition came out clearly for the introduction of political pluralism and a multiparty system. As a result of these differences. a considerable number of members left the League of Communists, reproaching the League for being vague, too slow, and not decisive enough in its endeavours for political pluralism and formal sovereignty. At the end of November 1989, the Slovene Government therefore allowed the introduction of a multiparty system in Slovenia in spite of opposition from the Federal Government, the Yugoslav army, and several of the other republics.

At the end of November with the unanimous support of the population, the Slovene Government banned a pan-Yugoslav demonstration that the centralist or rather Great Serbia forces from all Yugoslavia had planned for Ljubljana. Similar demonstrations had by then been organized everywhere in Yugoslavia except Slovenia and Croatia and had brought down autonomy-oriented republic governments, replacing them with adherents of centralism and allies of Slobodan Milošević. Serbia and Montenegro reacted to the ban by breaking off all commercial relations with Slovenia. At the end of 1989, the opposition coalition *Demos* was formed from several democratic opposition parties: the Slovene Democratic Union, the Social Democratic Union of Slovenia, the Slovene Farmers' Union, the Slovene Christian Democrats, and the Green Party of Slovenia. The coalition was formally presided over by the president of the Social Democratic Union, Dr. Jože Pučnik, who at the beginning of 1989 had returned from many years of living in Germany where he had gone because of the persecution of the Communist regime.

In January 1990, the Great Serbia hegemonic leanings which dominated the League of Communists of Yugoslavia led to the withdrawal of the members of the Slovene League of Communists from the Congress of the League of Communists of Yugoslavia in Belgrade and subsequently to withdraw entirely from the League of Communists of Yugoslavia. With this act the last remaining bond between the Slovenes and the federal Yugoslavia was broken.

The democratic elections for the Slovene Parliament in April 1990 brought a 55% victory for the *Demos* coalition while the remaining votes went to the three parties which were considered the heirs of the previous system even though they had also declared themselves in favour of a market economy and political democracy (the League of Communists of Slovenia received 17%; the Socialist Youth Party that on the eve of the elections adopted the name Liberal Democratic Party, 14%; and the Socialist Party established from the previous Socialist Union, 5.5%). The *Demos* government was formed by Lojze Peterle, the president of the strongest coalition party, the Slovene Christian Democrats. The most important ministries entrusted with organizing Slovenia's independence were given to the members of the Slovene Democratic Party: Dr. Dimitrij Rupel (Foreign Affairs), Janez Janša (Defense), and Igor Bavčar (Internal Affairs). The break with the old socialist regime proceeded peacefully, although at this break many Slovenes wanted to preserve some continuity with what had been good in the old regime including general employment and the high level of social security and equality. They saw a kind of guarantee for these achievements in Milan Kučan, the social democratic orientated former-President of the League of Communists of Slovenia, who during the second round of direct elections for President of the Presidency of the Republic of Slovenia won a clear victory with 59% of the votes against the *Demos* candidate Jože Pučnik who symbolized the political break.

25. Endeavours to Strengthen Democracy and the Independence of the Slovene State

By late spring of 1990, all the parties in the new democratically - constituted Slovene government had agreed on a platform of Slovene national and governmental independence within a Yugoslav confederation and were resolved to settle Slovenia's relationship to this union in a peaceful and democratic way by means of mutual agreement as soon as possible. Along with the possibility of confederation, Slovenia also offered a form of union of independent republics. However, neither the central government headed by Prime Minister Marković nor the Presidency of Yugoslavia as the representative of the Socialist Federal Republic of Yugoslavia nor the Federal Assembly were prepared to talk with Slovenia and Croatia about the transformation of the federation. At that time, Slovenia and Croatia were the only republics in which pluralist political democracy had been established, and therefore they appeared to be jointly involved in unraveling the Yugoslav knot, both inside Yugoslavia as well as in the eyes of the international public. When in the summer of 1990 the Great Serbia nationalists realized that the prospects for centralized and unchanged Yugoslavia were diminishing, they decided on a violent course to prevent the formation of a confederative Croatia (which would have solved the question of the Serbs in Croatia) and the eventual establishment of a Yugoslav confederation. With the help of the federal Yugoslav army, or rather its Great Serbia officer cadre, the Croatian Serbs in Lika and northern Dalmatia rose in direct armed revolt against the government of the Republic of Croatia. The political situation in Croatia moved closer to outright war, threatening also Slovenia and its aim of independence. The Federal Yugoslav government and the army attempted to disarm Slovenia's Territorial Defence Forces but did not succeed entirely.

Slovenia refused to be intimidated. It merely began considering international political and legal norms for declaring its independence, either through a constitutional act or through a plebiscite. In the autumn of 1990, the leadership of the governing *Demos* coalition presided over by Jože Pučnik suggested an all-nation plebiscite in Slovenia. In some circles this proposal first met with some skepticism, but the Slovene Parliament subsequently adopted a law on a plebiscite by acclamation and fixed December 23, 1990, for its implementation. The leadership of the Catholic Church headed by Ljubljana's Archbishop Šuštar also expressed its support for the plebiscite. The outcome was quite clear and unequivocal: of the 89% of eligible voters who participated, 90% voted for a free and independent Slovenia. When the result of the plebiscite was announced, it was followed by spontaneous all-nation rejoicing. The plebiscite statistics are proof that in addition to the votes of the Slovene majority, the votes of many members of other Yugoslav nationalities living in Slovenia contributed to such an overwhelming positive outcome. The plebiscite decision was therefore not a narrow nationalistic act in favour of a nationalistic Slovenia but a democratic decision by a great majority of the citizens of Slovenia who voted for an independent and democratic republic in which all citizens would enjoy the same rights regardless their origins.

After the outcome of the Slovene plebiscite was announced, the Republic of Serbia gained access illegally to the Yugoslav monetary system in early January 1991 and misappropriated almost the total planned monetary issue of the Yugoslav federation set aside for the year 1991. It became increasingly obvious that it would be difficult to achieve a confederative or any other agreement within Yugoslavia and that the Great Serbia nationalists headed by Milošević were prepared for everything. Also in their favour was the behaviour of the international community, including the United States, the European Community, and the Soviet Union, all of whom were interested in the further existence and unity of Yugoslavia and did not comprehend what was happening in Yugoslavia or why. They therefore did not support the transformation of the federation. Yugoslavia's Prime Minister Marković succeeded in presenting himself to the world as a liberal economic reformer and a conciliatory figure. He even succeeded in getting a guarantee of new loans. The Serbian generals at the top of the Yugoslav military and their adherents in Yugoslavia's diplomatic corps spoke loudly of a "fourth German Reich" which supposedly the independent republics of Slovenia and Croatia would immediately join.

Both Croatia and Slovenia decided on dates for the implementation of the decisions of their plebiscites. The confederative solution was withdrawing increasingly before harsh reality.

26. A Ten-Day War for the Independence and International Recognition of Slovenia

During the night following the ceremonies proclaiming the independence of the Republic of Slovenia on June 26, 1991, the Yugoslav Army, with the tacit agreement of the international community, went into action to try and quash the existence of the new independent state by force. The Slovenes responded as one to this violent act of the Yugoslav federal government and army through the organized resistance of the police and the Territorial Defence forces and spontaneous all-nation resistance which on the first day of the struggle largely succeeded in blocking the movement of Yugoslav army units. The Yugoslav army was not prepared for such resistance, and after several days of military action which cost forty-five lives and considerable material damage, army units began disintegrating and surrendering to Slovene Territorial Defence forces. These army units were composed largely of soldiers of non-Serbian nationalities who were unwilling to fight the Slovenes. Events appeared to be moving toward a complete and shameful military debacle. In order to avoid such a disaster, on the fourth day of the war army headquarters in Belgrade threatened Slovenia with the worst retaliatory measures, aerial bombardment and total war.

The Slovene government turned to the international public, a decisive political factor, pleading with them to prevent a great human tragedy and a blow to European civilization. Responding to the shocking pictures and reports of military devastations by the Yugoslav army sent into the world by numerous foreign correspondents as well as by the information service of the Slovene government, world public opinion quickly mobilized and demanded an end to the military intervention of the Yugoslav army. Truly generous humanitarian aid was offered to Slovenia by neighbouring countries. German Foreign Minister Genscher flew to Zagreb in haste, and on the seventh day of the war, a top-level political mission from the European Community consisting of three foreign ministers (Van den Broek from The Netherlands, de Michelis from Italy, and Santer from Luxembourg) also arrived in Zagreb. The mission mediated decisively in negotiations between the delegation of the Yugoslav federal government and army and the delegation of the Republic of Slovenia and succeeded in bringing about the end of military hostilities. Slovenia had to agree to a three-month moratorium on the implementation of its indepen-dence and in this period to try and achieve recognition of its independence through negotiation. This decision was just: the war was over. Slovenia kept its independence.

Several days later, negotiations continued between the hostile parties on the island of Brioni with the mediation of the three ministers from the European Community. They endorsed the agree-ment made in Zagreb on a three-month moratorium with the assurance that the European Community would then recognize the independence of Slovenia. Immediately after this assurance was given, the Yugoslav delegation astounded everyone with its decision to withdraw the Yugoslav army from Slovenia within three months. With minor delays, this was actually accomplished by the autumn of 1991. Thus Slovenia became a sovereign state in fact with its government the sole authority. On December 28, 1991, the new Constitution of the Republic of Slovenia was adopted. In the international arena, however, more battles had to be won before Slovenia would be internationally recognized. In its struggle for international recognition, Slovenia was most firmly supported by Germany, Austria, Hungary, Czechoslovakia, and Poland. Several other European countries including Italy, France, and Great Britain eventually concurred, and the Vatican also offered significant public support. Although some members of the European Community tried to delay recognition, in mid-December the decision was made at a European Community conference to recognize independent Slovenia and Croatia on January 15, 1992. Several European and non-European countries recognized Slovenia even earlier.

In the spring of 1992, disagreements concerning the laws on privatization, denationalization, social policy, education, the role and influence of the Catholic Church, and making amends for injustices done in the past were so great within the *Demos* coalition that it simply disintegrated. A new coalition government in which there were several *Demos* parties and former opposition parties was formed by the president of the Liberal Democratic Party, Dr. Janez Drnovšek.

On May 22, 1992, Slovenia was admitted to the United Nations as a full member.

TABLE OF CONTENTS

Dr. Janko Prunk
A BRIEF HISTORY OF SLOVENIA

Foreword by
Borut Šuklje

Translated by
Wayne Tuttle
Majda Klander

Cover by
Jurij Kocbek

Published by
ZALOŽBA GRAD

Editor
Alenka Štante

Printed by
SOMARU Ljubljana

Po mnenju Ministrstva za kulturo št. 415-508/96 se za knjigo plačuje davek od prometa proizvodov po stopnji 5%.

ISBN 961-90119-2-9